Bonfire of the Cer
the second human 1

Cliff Slaughter

Copyright © 2013

All rights reserved. No part of this book may be reproduced, stored, or transmitted by any means—whether auditory, graphic, mechanical, or electronic—without written permission of both publisher and author, except in the case of brief excerpts used in critical articles and reviews. Unauthorized reproduction of any part of this work is illegal and is punishable by law.

ISBN 978-1-291-21321-8

Contents

Preface vii
Introduction xiii

Chapter 1 Humanity's crisis ... and beyond 1
           (a) 'Destructive self-reproduction' of capital ....
           (b) Economy and ecology – a single crisis ....
           (c) Twentieth-century changes in capitalism ....
           (d) An interruption! ....
           (e) The structural crisis of capital and the class
               struggle ....
           (f) Agency – the issues ....

Chapter 2 'Overdeveloped' countries and
           'underdevelopment' 24
           (a) Two sides to overdevelopment ....
           (b) Overdevelopment and 'underdevelopment' ....
           (c) Changes in the working class ....

Chapter 3 Overdevelopment has pathological results 37
           (a) Overdevelopment and the condition of the
               working class ....
           (b) Overdeveloped capital is criminal – some
               examples ....
           (c) Waking from the nightmare ....
           (d) Capital has bolted ....

Chapter 4 Socialisation of production, and communism 47
           (a) The potential of forces of production ....

	(b) Socialisation of production, precondition of socialism ....
	(c) The 'social brain' ....
	(d) The social brain confined ....
Chapter 5	About time – and free time 63
	(a) 'All real economy is economy of time' ....
	(b) Free time ....
	(c) 'The annihilation of space by time' ....
Chapter 6	Human labour and its future 71
	(a) Living labour and 'dead labour' ....
	(b) Labour and communism ....
Chapter 7	Individuals 81
	(a) The individual and 'real wealth' ....
	(b) The conditions for 'universally developed individuals' ....
Chapter 8	The 'human revolution' … and the modern family? 87
	(a) Crisis of the modern family ....
	(b) From the first 'human revolution' to the second ....
	(c) Has the family a future? ....
	(d) Note: some opinions on the family and marriage ....
Chapter 9	Revolutionary agency: the theoretical framework..101
Chapter 10	Defending the future 107
	(a) The future under threat ....
	(b) How to begin the defence? ....
	(c) 'Oppositional public space' ....

Chapter 11	Ends and means	121
	(a) The necessity of a clear understanding of the end	
	(b) Against 'the end justifies the means'	
	(c) Class-consciousness; class and party	
	(d) A working 'stitched up'	
Chapter 12	Utopias … and a way forward?	141
	(a) Some past utopias	
	(b) Is our vision of the future utopian? And Guadeloupe	
	(c) A way forward - utopian?	
Chapter 13	About art and beauty	161
Chapter 14	By way of conclusions	175

Preface

This book will be thought over-ambitious, in that it attacks the great and difficult problems of how humanity can, indeed must, escape the historical, social, economic and ecological crises facing us, and of where is the force which will be able to do this. At the same time, the book should be seen as a self-criticism, in that I will say clearly that – I speak for myself – some of us Marxists did not hold sufficiently fast to the need always to put the truth first, above all temporary considerations. We owe to Harold Pinter the firmest and most passionate affirmation of this necessity:

> I believe that, despite the enormous odds which exist, unflinching, unswerving, fierce intellectual determination, as citizens, to define the real truth of our lives and our societies is a crucial obligation which devolves upon us all. It is, in fact, mandatory. If such a determination is not embodied in our political vision, we have no hope of restoring what is so nearly lost to us – the dignity of man. (Nobel Lecture, 2005)

This short book is dedicated to the memory of my comrade and friend Peter Fryer, who lived by that truth.

The arrival of the capitalist system, in our day, at its stage of 'destructive self-reproduction', threatening to destroy the natural and human foundations of a future positive society, surely forces us to acknowledge the narrowness of our own past conceptions (too narrowly 'economic', too narrowly 'political') of the struggle for social emancipation. The great novelist D.H.Lawrence was no socialist, but his vision was profound. He reflected on his youthful cooperation with Middleton Murry in a small anti-war magazine of 1915, in a passage which may sound to some pessimistic in its realism, but is essentially optimistic. He wrote:

> I can't believe in 'doing things' like that. In a great issue like the war, there was nothing to be 'done' in Murry's sense. There is still nothing to be 'done'. Probably not for many, many years will men start to 'do something. And even then, only after they have changed gradually, and deeply.
>
> I knew then, and I know now, it is no use trying to do anything – I speak only for myself – publicly. It is no use trying merely to modify present forms. The whole great form of our era will have to go. And nothing will really send it down but the new shoots of life springing up and slowly bursting the foundations. And one can do nothing, but fight tooth and nail to defend the new shoots of life from being crushed out, and let them grow. We can't make life. We can but fight for the life that grows in us. ('Reflections on the Death of a Porcupine and Other Essays', in *Phoenix II: Uncollected, unpublished and other prose works by D. H Lawrence*, Viking Press, 1968, p. 364)

His contemporary, Italian revolutionary Antonio Gramsci, was in a country and in a situation where it indeed was possible to 'do something'. He wrote in his journal *Ordine Nuovo* in 1919:

> It is necessary, with bold spirit and in good conscience, to save civilisation. We must halt the dissolution which corrodes and corrupts the roots of human society. The bare and barren tree can be made green again.
>
> Are we not ready?

There could be no better clarion call for what I am trying to say in this book. The resolution of this crisis of human civilisation depends on this 'halting the dissolution which corrodes and corrupts the roots of human society.' We have to pose the question: does it remain true that the achievement of a truly internationalist working-class movement which can overcome the defeats and betrayals of the past as well as the divisions in the world's working class which have resulted from imperialism and globalisation is central to this task? However that question is answered, it is a task which will and must be shared, in new ways, with millions of others who find themselves faced with the necessity of acting against the prevailing barbarism. It is to this end that the following chapters are directed.

Acknowledgments

I am indebted to many comrades for help in striving to understand the problems discussed in this book, and in particular Istvan Meszaros, whose influence is, I hope, apparent. The final preparation of the text owes everything to Hilary Horrocks.

Introduction

A brief description of how this book came to have its present form should help to underline the fact that it is intended to be not 'the finished article' but a contribution to a vitally necessary discussion. Initially, I had found myself more and more preoccupied by the problem of time. The 'information revolution' reduces to an infinitesimal amount the time needed not only for communication (at any distance: a friend reminded me of Marx's 'the annihilation of space by time') but also for production and its control (here again Marx, who cited the classical economists' 'the only real economy is economy of time'). This, it seemed to me, must have enormous implications for the whole system of production and the social life based upon it, most of all because that system, dominated by capital and its imperatives, depends fundamentally on the value produced in the labour-time of workers. In trying to develop a Marxist understanding of the present, we need to bear in mind always Marx's own insistence that any part of a system or structure can be understood only from the standpoint of the nature of its whole. And today's 'globalised' whole is much changed from Marx's day, so that the understanding of the parts of the capital system has to be reworked, rather than relying solely on Marx's own characterisations.

Furthermore, the vastly increased productivity of labour not only greatly enhances the accumulation of surplus value by capital but also reduces greatly the labour-time necessary to meet human needs. This means that an unheard-of amount of free, disposable time can be available to men and women. The implications of this, so long as capital controls production (unemployment, casualisation, diminution of the proportion of the workforce engaged in manufacturing, etc) are clear, but we are led at the same time to return to what it can mean for a future, different form of society. The prospect of free, disposable time for everyone in a socialist/communist society, where 'the free development of each is the condition of the free development of all', with all individuals having access to the riches of the world's cultures and able to exercise their own talents and creativity, must then be discussed.

The impact of these great changes in our 'globalised' society is extremely uneven. Many millions, even billions, live in dire poverty and without the most basic requirements of daily living in the 'underdeveloped countries' of Africa, Asia and Latin America.[1] Yet the countries of Western Europe, North America and Japan are what I have here called 'overdeveloped countries' (I explain in the early chapters the exact sense in which I use this term). The original draft was modified to concentrate on and begin from this overdevelopment and its social-pathological consequences, and its origins in the basic character of capitalist production.

At the same time, pursuing the implications of 'free, disposable time' and the kind of society in which it could form the basis of a truly human existence, I repeatedly came back to Marx's characterisation of the necessary social revolution as 'the human revolution'. More and more, this appeared to me, however general, even abstract, to be the most basic and comprehensive category and theme, embracing all else. For this reason I posed the question of a second 'human revolution', like the first human revolution (the transition from pre-human to human and the origins of culture) but overcoming the dehumanisation imposed by the oppressive and exploitative social systems of more recent history (forms of oriental despotism in the Near East and India; slavery and feudalism in Europe; and finally the rule of capital, which soon became a global system), and at the same time appropriating, this time for all, the historic conquests of humanity's cultures.

At this stage it was therefore proposed to start from the meaning of 'human revolution', concentrating on the family, its origins and its contemporary crisis. In discussion of this proposed treatment of the book's content, it was pointed out to me that the

---

[1] 'The Millennium Development Goal of eradicating hunger by 2015 will not be achieved', Robert B. Zoellick 'Pursuing more growth in an uncertain world', in *The Express Tribune*, 18 September 2010
'After falling in the previous decade, poverty and malnutrition rates began to rise again in 2008 and the World Bank estimates that 64 million more people are living in extreme poverty in 2010' (*Le Monde Diplomatique*, October 2010)

relationship between its several themes and components did not emerge sufficiently clearly, and that this might be overcome by starting – very concretely, so to speak – with the patently critical state of the world situation in which we find ourselves, posing as clearly as possible the question of alternatives to the present order and how they might be achieved.

Here a note on method is in order. However straightforward the latter choice of starting-point seemed to be, I had to bear in mind the axiom that the truly concrete is only arrived at through a series of abstract concepts, if a 'false' (superficial) concrete is to be avoided. Marx noted in his *Grundrisse* that, contrary to common sense, 'human anatomy contains a key to the anatomy of the ape' (p. 105). To understand the meaning of something past, it is necessary to start from what the thing has now become.

With this in mind, should we not say that a book like this should not be (a) 'looking at the present crisis of humanity from the standpoint of Marxism', but (b) 'looking critically at Marx's work from the standpoint of the present crisis of humanity'?!

To re-frame this question: 'Are the writings of Marx, or Marxism at its present stage of development, adequate as a theory to understand the present crisis?' rather than (as is common) 'Let's look at Marx's writings to see if there are theoretical guidelines for understanding the present crisis?' The latter procedure might well prove to a certain extent useful, but it fails to take into account the dialectical interrelation between a and b above. To put it more simply: the 'anatomy of man – anatomy of the ape' dictum is necessary for both the world situation 2011/1848-65 and Marxism 2011/Marx 1848-65.

Surely most important here is that our present historical (structural) crisis of capital constitutes a dire threat to the very future existence of human culture, even of human life itself (destruction of the environment, natural and built). This threat – recognised by millions – can be removed only by a massive social change, a revolution.

We are propelled back, then, to Marx's insistence that the proletarian revolution he foresaw would be, must be, the human revolution, a revolution opening up a truly human future, overcoming the inhumanity of capital's rule already apparent to Marx as to many others a century and a half ago. Hence our insistence in this book on the meaning of 'the human revolution'.

So much for starting from the present crisis in beginning to understand the past. What about starting from the point of development reached today by Marxism since Marx? This side of the problem is more controversial. In the context of the problems dealt with in the present work, I strongly suggest that at present we must take István Mészáros' work, and especially his *Beyond Capital*, as the most developed and comprehensive understanding of Marxist theory. There we find a critical analysis of the only substantial twentieth-century Marxist work on class-consciousness (Georg Lukács; see chapters on this subject below). The most important Marxists of the last century were Lenin and Trotsky. Some would-be Marxists hold that Lenin's *Imperialism, the highest stage of capitalism* is still the key to our epoch, even though it has been left behind by history. More important for our purposes is the way in which his writings on leadership and class-consciousness, developed in conditions of Tsarist oppression and illegality, were taken by Communist Parties all over the world to be the recipe for 'vanguard parties' in all conditions. Trotsky wrote brilliantly and led the principled fight against the Stalinist distortion of Lenin's heritage, but his notions of leadership, party and the nature of the epoch now need a thoroughly critical review. Mészáros makes the clearest case for a renewal of Marxism: his reaffirmation of the revolutionary role of the working class, however, poses the most difficult question of all – how in practice will this social agency necessary to put an end to the rule of capital be prepared, forged, organised?

Thus from these methodological considerations it became crystal-clear that the most critical question of all, and the most difficult, is that of 'agency': who will act to initiate the necessary fundamental historical changes? That is to say: besides the question of what elements of a future society are promised and prepared by the material changes in present-day economy and society, there remains the question: who, what social force, with what kind of organisation and action, with what kind of politics, will be able to challenge and overturn the rule of capital? Old answers to this question must be critically reviewed, and existing movements and actions questioned and learned from. A frank and objective conclusion concerning the possibility of finding answers that take fully into account the great social and economic changes of the last hundred years will be necessary. Our aim cannot be to provide the answers, only to put the discussion on a firmer basis.

It is for these reasons that this book works towards this most difficult problem of all. The question of 'agency' is introduced in the first chapter, in the context of the present historical crisis of the system, a crisis manifested in economy, politics, social conditions and in the deadly threat to our natural environment. I return to aspects of this matter of agency at several points in the subsequent chapters, and finally devote the longest section of the book to its detailed treatment.

Chapter 1

Humanity's crisis ... and beyond

These are the days of miracle and wonder,
This is a long-distance call ...

('Boy in the Bubble', song by Paul Simon, 1986)

We can agree; and the miraculous advances in the means of production and communication achieved since the song was written, with their obvious potential of abundance and universal intercourse, go far beyond what Paul Simon saw, and far, far beyond what Karl Marx could have envisaged a century and a half ago. The material means are there for all human individuals to have the free time to develop their creative potential. The globalisation of capital and the communications revolution created by information technology (internet, etc) could open up the whole world and the cultures of all its peoples to every individual.

And yet this promise is not fulfilled. On the contrary, we see billions of human beings living in dire poverty, and countless thousands killed or maimed in wars. Just one statistic (of the many which could be cited) tells all: one child in the world dies of starvation every five seconds!

Future generations will look back on our times and see as the height of madness (of men and women ruled by capital and its needs) the fact that the enormous potential of productivity and communication could not be directed by the people of the 'advanced' capitalist countries to the burning needs of the rest of the world (or even of their own poor). The social order necessary to capital's rule and the accompanying ideological wasteland combine to make such an elementary human/communal response unthinkable. Margaret Thatcher's 'There is no alternative' was the brutally naïve affirmation of this inhumanity. The crushing out of elementary human mutual sympathy and mutual aid has centuries of conditioning behind it. The ability of men and women to still feel and act with human kindness in their individual lives despite this conditioning is a precious resource for the coming struggles to change the world.

The crying contradiction between promise and reality is not due to the greed of bankers or to the mistakes or inabilities of statesmen or anyone else. It arises from the very nature of the social system in which we live. It is a contradiction that will be overcome only when that system itself is overcome. And here we meet the most difficult question: how will the system be overcome? How can humanity emerge from the present economic, political and environmental crises? And, most problematical of all, who, what social force, will effect this change, and by what means?

More than a century and a half ago, a clear answer was given by the young Marx and Engels in their *Communist Manifesto* (1847). Against the rule of capital, they concluded: 'Workers of all countries, unite! You have nothing to lose but your chains!' This has been the watchword of revolutionary socialists up to our own day. We need urgently to critically review it in the light of the greatly changed situation globally and nationally. In the light of the many changes since Marx's day, does it still make sense to see the working class as a potentially revolutionary force? Are there now forms of resistance and other social forces that can have that role?

First, let us see why Marx arrived at his conclusion. It is capital and its needs that determine the functioning of the existing social order. Capital (which is of course the product of past labour, appropriated by capitalists) depends on the existence of a class of men and women who, having no means of production of their own, individually or collectively, have no other choice than to sell their labour-power for wages. Once their labour-power is bought and put to work under the control of its purchaser, it becomes labour. To have this mass of labour-power available for purchase, capitalism had to begin, centuries ago, with the forcible theft of all means of production (land, etc) from the communities and individuals who had depended on them.

Having been sold to the capitalist, the worker's labour-power becomes the property of the purchaser, the employer, just as does any other commodity, to be used by the buyer according to his needs. Capital pays for labour-power (wages) – enough to keep the worker until he must return for another day; but the worker's labour actually produces a value in excess of what is paid for his labour-power. This excess is surplus-value which, when the product is sold, is 'realised' by the capitalist as profit and accumulated as capital.

This mode of exploitation has been the case for the centuries of capitalism's existence and ascendancy. Until our own day, capital's unquenchable thirst for accumulation had a progressive historical role, in that it led to an unprecedented development of mankind's productive forces and the opening up of relations between all parts of the world (the world market). It was for this reason that Marx could know that capitalism prepares the material preconditions for a socialist society. Marx saw the working class or proletariat as the structural antagonist of capital, that is to say, structurally necessary to capital, but with its interests diametrically opposed to it.

Now, are there not new and massive problems today standing in the way of an international 'unity' of the workers of all countries against globalised capital?

And can it any longer be said that the workers have 'nothing to lose but their chains'?

And if the prospect of working-class unity and revolutionary action is changed by the answers to these questions, then what kind of social force, and with what methods, can confront the power of capital and fundamentally change the world, rescuing humanity from the threats to our future posed by the continued uncontrolled rule of capital? This is the great problem of 'agency'.

These questions will recur in various aspects throughout the following chapters. In the first place, before examining the alternatives to be considered, it is surely necessary to try to examine more closely the stage now reached by capitalism and to ask what lies behind the changes in economy and society since the nineteenth century. And, at least as important, a critique (including a self-criticism) of the past theory and practice of those who have been in the leadership of the working-class movement, or have aspired to replace that leadership, often 'taking for granted' the lasting validity of Marx's 1847 conclusion, is essential.

(a) The 'destructive self-reproduction' of capital

What are the most important of these changes, and what changes in our ideas must follow? One of the bedrock concepts for a socialist theory that is not merely utopian has been that industrial capitalism and its need for a world market develop the objective material conditions for a socialist society. We now must understand that the limits of that progressive historical role have now been reached, and passed. So advanced now are the productive forces, and so immediately perceptible the possibility of universal intercourse between humans of all countries on the planet, that a system (the rule of capital) that rests on 'the theft of alien labour time' (Marx), with its resulting necessary accumulation of capital, can no longer be progressive in any sense but becomes literally reactionary. Despite the dreadful uncontrolled plundering (to the point of exhaustion) of vital natural resources, despite the now universally recognised threat of extreme degradation of the environment, despite the ever-asserted necessity of brutal wars to maintain capital's control of every part of the world and its resources, the drive for profit and accumulation is as inexorable as ever. The means which now make possible a truly human 'universal intercourse' are perverted. They are a means of universal exploitation, speculation, destruction, war. By 2009 technological advance had made possible 'drone' (i.e. pilotless) aircraft – they are used for bombing expeditions and for the surveillance of would-be immigrants. So much for the meaning of 'universal intercourse' for the owners of labour-power, in contrast to the free movement of capital globally.

The undeniable fact is that the time left for humanity's continued existence on earth is under threat, yet capital drives ahead, concerned only with the time that can profitably be taken from the worker. The quantity of that time (a quantity stolen from the lifetime of the worker), and the quantity of the capital which can be thereby accumulated, are all that count. This predominates over all considerations of the quality of the individual workers' lives, the quality of the environment, and the quality of the goods produced. What is a man worth? For capital, the answer depends only on the amount of labour-time that can be taken from him. 'Time is everything, man is nothing; he is at the most time's carcase. Quality no longer matters. Quantity alone decides everything; hour for hour; day for day.'[2]

Thus it is of no consequence what is produced and of what quality, so long as it contains surplus value which can be realised on the market. It should come as no surprise that the production of what amounts to waste on an ever-increasing scale has become essential to capital's mode of existence. A product that is wasted, or quickly worn out, or even systematically destroyed in massive quantities, as with weapons of war, is of no less 'value' (i.e. exchange value, which can be realised at a profit), than any useful product. More and more, capital needs this production of soon-to-be-destroyed, soon-to-be-used up, soon-obsolete goods, which must then be replaced, just as it needs a mass consumer market in the 'advanced' countries, if the profit on transnational companies' investment in dirt-cheap labour in Asia is to be 'realised'.

And here, an additional insoluble contradiction of the capital system in our day comes into play. The promise of universal intercourse, mutual aid and cooperation which globalisation of capital foreshadows cannot at this time be even partially fulfilled, because the global economy (profit-oriented, based on the hierarchical control of labour and the division into antagonistic classes) has no political equivalent to enable regulation of its social antagonisms. That is, there is no state or government congruent with the now global economy. When, in the past, capital's role was historically progressive (above) the nation-state was the political framework within which each national capitalist class could find ways of controlling or attenuating the social conflicts generated by capitalist exploitation, and regulating to some extent the relation between competing capitals. Now there is no equivalent, no state to correspond to the global economy, which is the playing-field of mighty transnational corporations.

---

[2] Marx, *The Poverty of Philosophy*, in Marx and Engels *Collected Works*, Vol 6, Lawrence & Wishart, 1976, pp. 126-7

István Mészáros sums up the implications of this non-equivalence for the social and political problems of the overdeveloped countries:

> In view of the fact that the most intractable of the global capital system's contradictions is the one between the internal unrestrainability of its economic constituents and the now inescapable necessity of introducing major restraints, any hope of finding a way out of this vicious circle under the circumstances marked by the activation of capital's absolute limits must be vested in the political dimension of the system ... the full powers of the state will be activated to serve the end of squaring capital's vicious circle, even if it means subjecting all potential dissent to extreme authoritarian constraints.[3]

Each nation-state competes (on behalf of its capitalist class) for influence or control over resources and avenues of investment. Such permanently potential conflict led in the past to the horrendous imperialist wars of the twentieth century. Today, the dominant power, the United States, strives by whatever means available to become itself the overall 'state' to match the economy of globalised capital. That is the reason for its continual military interventions (Iraq, Afghanistan, etc) as well as its ruthless economic subjugation of any territory which it can dominate, and its role in imposing military dictatorships (Indonesia) and overthrowing elected governments (Chile).

This attempt by the United States ruling class to rule the world as if it were the political state required by the international economy is inevitably doomed to failure. How, for example, can it withstand or contain the emergence of China and India as great powers economically and politically? Contained in this contradiction is the inevitability, so long as capital rules, of humanly disastrous confrontations and conflicts, added to the already growing threat posed by the blind drive for profit without regard for damage to nature and it resources and the consequent threat to the future of humanity.

The fact is that capital, always characterised by periodic financial, commercial and industrial crises, has now entered the period

---

[3] István Mészáros, *Beyond Capital*, Merlin Press, 1995, p. 146

of a different crisis, its crisis as a system, its crisis as the structure and life-process of society, thus its historical crisis, its structural crisis.

In the simplest terms: the survival of capital's rule stands in stark contradiction to the survival of humanity. And the necessity of asserting humanity's self-control over our own work and over all the conquests of our own labour (that is, a communist or socialist order of free and equal individuals) demands that we find ways to end the rule of capital.

The era of structural crisis that opened up in the last quarter of the twentieth century will contain within itself all manner of periodic economic (especially financial) and political crises. In the course of time, the problems of falling standards of living, unemployment, decline of health and housing facilities, care for the elderly and the young, and the inevitable convergence of the problems of the oppressed in all parts of the world, must provoke resistance and new forms of organising that resistance. The social, moral and educational damage wrought by the structural crisis, and the latter's increasingly evident threat to human existence, will bring together men and women from all walks of life, from scientists, artists and writers to the most deprived people. It is clear that to be effective, a spatial coordination and temporal continuity will be necessary. Because of the multiformity of the issues raised by a structural crisis which embraces every aspect of society and culture, the social composition and forms of organisation of movements of protest and resistance will be new and very varied.

The relation of these movements to the working class is something that will have to be discovered/invented, and it must be recognised that the existing traditional organisations of the working class (trade unions, political parties) are not fitted for the task. On the contrary, the working class is politically disenfranchised, with the Labour, socialist and social-democratic parties having abandoned even their reformist, class-collaborationist role of earlier years. They are no longer working-class parties (even in the sense of the British Labour Party being a 'general association of the working class', as Lenin once characterised it), regardless of how many workers vote for them. As for the Communist Parties, they had since the advent of Stalinism been little more than instruments of Soviet foreign policy, in which Stalin's 'peaceful coexistence' with capitalism meant the end of any revolutionary policies, with descent into the mysteries of 'socialism in a single country' and 'peaceful, parliamentary roads to socialism' (the latter an extraordinary abandonment of the patent truth that electoral democracy without social and economic equality of the voters is no democracy at all, if democracy really does mean 'rule by the people').

Trade unions in Britain and other countries have been crippled by anti-union legislation (endorsed and acted upon by the British Labour Party in government). These unions now organise only a small minority of workers, and only a militant opposition, overturning the existing leaderships and their virtual integration into the state, could possibly make them once again effective. We shall see a revived working-class movement only through a fight to build new and extra-parliamentary instruments of struggle which are able to merge with and learn from movements and protests on issues and with initial aims which do not begin as explicitly socialist or working-class at all. It is the unrealisability of their demands within the capitalist order, something learned in struggle, with setbacks and disappointments as well as partial gains, that is decisive. It is thus the responsibility of socialists to study and to connect with every form of resistance and organisation, and to proceed always from the fight to meet people's needs, in no way trying to dictate from outside, and certainly not from above, to the real movement. As we shall see, this responsibility entails a thorough settlement with our past conceptions of 'revolutionary leadership'.

In summary, there is an inescapable conclusion. The capital system's fundamental dependence on the exploitation of wage-labour ('the theft of alien labour-time', Marx) for its self-reproduction makes it no longer in any way progressive but reactionary and destructive. By destructive here is meant: the conquests of science become destructive, perverted by capital, so that instead of delivering to humanity the material and cultural wealth promised by today's productive forces and means of communication, they now produce degradation, waste, war, because these evils enable the production and 'realisation' of surplus value, profit and the accumulation of capital on a massive scale.

Like other great writers, Albert Camus had profound insight into our condition, a condition in which the working men and women in history are reduced to being anonymous victims of what is actually their own creation, appropriated by capital and used to exploit them:

> There was a mystery about that man, a mystery he had wanted to penetrate. But after all there was only the mystery of poverty that creates beings without names and without a past, that sends them into the vast throng of *the nameless dead who made the world* [my emphasis, CS] while they themselves were destroyed for ever.

And:

> 'Rescue this poor family from the fate of the poor, which is to disappear from history without a trace.'[4]

(b) Economy and ecology: a single crisis

How should socialists respond to the fact (more and more obvious and recognised) that capital's ruthless drive for profit and capital accumulation brings us nearer to the brink of a natural and human disaster?

Certainly it is tempting to write, as some Marxists have done, of 'joint crises' of ecology and of the economy, and to emphasise the point that socialists must address both.[5] However, if we seek ways of doing the latter, it is necessary to clarify as best we can the real nature of these 'crises'.

I suggest that we should be thinking in terms of a single crisis: thus, the ecological crisis is the threat of destruction of essential elements of the natural environment on which human life depends. Where does this threat come from? Its cause is not natural. Natural disasters here face humanity for a non-natural reason. Simply put, it is the imperative of accumulation by competing capitals that has led to nature's resources being plundered with no regard whatsoever for the consequences for the

---

[4] Albert Camus, *The First Man*, Penguin, 1996, pp. 150-1 and 238
[5] Cf. François Chesnais, 'L'intrusion de Gaia' in *Carré Rouge*, No. 41, June 2009, p. 35

natural environment. Nature is exploited, plundered, rather than husbanded. The global reach of capital, first commercial then industrial, achieved over the last century and more, takes not the slightest account of the combined results of this exploitation. The 'ecological crisis' is the ultimate manifestation of the imperatives of the capital system.

This destruction of nature has now reached a critical point, having accelerated at a rate which has shocked, despite the warnings of scientists over the years. The underlying question here is: what historical point of development has the capital system, responsible for the 'ecological crisis', now reached? At this point, a brief historical sketch will begin to show the implications of the changes taking place over the last century for our problem of how the present historical crisis is to be overcome.

(c) Twentieth-century changes in capitalism

Already before the end of the nineteenth century, capitalism had entered the stage in which every corner of the world fell within its sphere of exploitation. To commercial domination of the world market was added the export of capital and establishment of manufacturing in the colonial and semi-colonial countries. The resources gained from this new imperialism were the foundation of capitalism's ability, in the twentieth century, to temporarily overcome its contradictions by displacing them, 'exporting' them, postponing them. It was possible in the richest countries to stave off working-class discontent and opposition by making economic and social concessions and reforms. Working-class solidarity was undermined by the inequalities between higher- and lower-paid workers. The essential internationalism of the working-class movement was undermined by the super-exploitation of colonial and semi-colonial labour, with workers in the metropolitan countries being better off economically and politically than their brothers and sisters in Asia, Africa and Latin America.

Based primarily on the better-off workers, working-class political parties went over to class-collaboration, opportunism and social-chauvinism, more and more tied to the capitalist state. The ruling classes of European countries even found it necessary and possible from time to time to 'rule through' social-democratic and labour governments. Once the German Social-Democrats had betrayed and then bloodily suppressed the revolution of 1919, murdering its leaders like Rosa Luxemburg, the isolation of the Russian October Revolution was inevitable, an isolation which led inexorably to the rise of Stalinism. Capital then had a priceless ally in the Stalinist bureaucracy, which disorientated and betrayed the millions of workers who formed Communist Parties throughout the world.

These economic and political changes in the late nineteenth and early twentieth centuries marked the beginning of an entirely new phase in the struggle of classes, a phase lasting through most of the twentieth century and leaving its mark on that struggle today. The relations between the working classes of Europe on the one hand and the peoples of the rest of the world could never be the same again. US capitalism, with the largest working class in the world, had begun its rapid rise to supremacy over Britain and Western Europe. The export of capital from the 'advanced capitalist countries' was changing class relations everywhere, so that as well as a world market, there was now a growing working class in countries like Russia. From this 'uneven development' there sprang explosive 'combined' results, with a newborn proletariat rapidly growing in the midst of semi-feudal and autocratic conditions. In Russia, Marxists like Lenin and Trotsky saw the proletariat, a small minority of the population, as the revolutionary force to overthrow the Tsarist autocracy.

The Great War of 1914-18 so undermined the Tsarist regime that it fell to the revolutions of 1917. The October Bolshevik revolution initiated a new stage in the international relations of the working class and in the development of the working-class political movement. Russia had a politically advanced working class, but the Bolshevik victory was achieved in a backward country. To go forward from revolution to the building of socialism was impossible until, in Lenin's words, 'the workers of the advanced capitalist countries come to our aid'. That did not happen. When, in the aftermath of military defeat (1919), there came a revolutionary insurrection by the German working class, it became immediately clear that the class's traditional (social-democratic) leadership had abandoned its Marxist foundations and gone over to the politics of compromise with capitalism. The SDP government turned the guns on the workers and butchered their leaders.

The inevitable consequences of the isolation of the Soviet system are familiar: Stalin and his allies were to pronounce that 'socialism in a single country' could and must be achieved, and the Communist International, founded in every country after October 1917 to bring together the newly-formed Communist Parties, was effectively turned from an instrument of revolution into an agency for (hopefully) neutralising the capitalist powers. As a direct result, the inter-war revolutions in China and Spain, and even the British 1926 General Strike, were deprived of the strategy, tactics and revolutionary organisation necessary for success. In the Soviet Union itself, the Stalinist terror killed off the old Bolshevik leaders, and millions died as all opposition was crushed. Trotsky's attempt to rally opposition to Stalin was met with exile, then with assassination.

In 1933, Hitler's Nazi Party came to power, and the German and Austrian working-class movements were crushed, a fate already met by the Italian working class at the hands of Mussolini's Fascism. Fascist success in Spain was to follow, when the Franco regime emerged victorious from the Spanish Civil War. Such was the condition of the working class in Western Europe when the 1939 War broke out.

The Second World War and the post-war reconstruction boom were the ways in which capitalism was able to displace or postpone its inner contradictions (which had been brutally revealed in the 1929 Wall Street crash and the Great Depression of the 1930s) and enter a new expansionary phase. After 1945, in the leading capitalist countries, reform concessions were made in response to working-class determination never to return to the 'Hungry Thirties', and the 'Welfare State' was born.

The surge of national liberation movements and the achievement of national independence by most colonial countries soon entered this changing picture. With the exception of China (soon followed by North Korea, Cambodia, Vietnam and Cuba), these newly independent countries remained in the capitalist orbit, with working classes, to be sure, but with a majority of peasants and petty producers. Despite the 'Marxist' pronouncements of many African leaders, these countries, from South Africa's and

Senegal's initial promise of democracy to Indonesia, are now corrupt dictatorships, 'brokering' capital from Europe and America. The 'communist' regimes of China, Korea and South-East Asia were in fact totalitarian dictatorships exploiting state property, able soon to make an easy transition to the capitalist regime of today.

Of first importance here is that China, with its workforce of billions, is now already rivalling the US as a capitalist power. In India also there is a hundreds-of-millions class of wage-workers. The way in which capitalism has come about and developed in China is historically unique, so that it is too early to say what institutional forms will take shape. Similarly, we cannot yet know what forms of organisation and resistance, industrial and political, will be found necessary and possible by these workers and others who confront these new forms of capitalism and capitalist rule. But what is certain is that it would be worse than dogmatic to cling to the notion that any victory they are able to achieve will have to await the 'workers of the advanced capitalist countries coming to their aid'. Indeed, as we shall argue in what follows, the working class in Europe and America has been to a great extent so 'stitched up', politically, economically and ideologically, that we may well see that relationship reversed.

It is certain that the severe attacks and cuts consequent on the unfolding of capital's structural crisis (attacks first becoming manifest in 2010 in response to the massive 'sovereign debt' problem in Europe and in the United States) will provoke a renewal of strike movements and even of trade unionism itself; and we must expect explosive social-revolutionary movements and outbreaks to occur in the 'emerging' countries like China, where masses of people are working for wages far, far lower than those of their counterparts in Western Europe, the United Sates and Japan, and as yet without the democratic rights which are supposed to prevail in those countries. The working class there is an awakening giant. Already motor manufacturers Honda and Toyota, manufacturing in China, have suffered lengthy strike actions. Following anger after a series of suicides caused by working conditions at the Foxconn (Taiwanese electronics giant) plant in China, the firm raised wages by 70 per cent in June 2010. In Bangladesh (22 June 2010) police had to fend off some 50,000 women workers demanding a threefold rise in their minimum wage of £17 per month. How long can the cheap labour of hundreds of millions in Asia last, especially given the deep concern of the Chinese rulers about the sharply declining birth-rate and the prospect of a severe labour shortage?

This changed relationship between the working class/working-class movements of Europe/USA and China/Asia (and probably Latin America and Africa) means that much of the argument in the following chapters can rightly be criticised as one-sided, since it tends to concentrate on social, economic and political problems in the older capitalist countries. At all points, therefore, allowances should be made for what is said here about the greatly changed and changing relationships within the working class of the world.

(d) An interruption!

Our understanding of these changes was rudely interrupted – and surely enormously enhanced – in the early months of 2011 by the eruption of mass movements in North Africa

In discussing the prospects internationally of resistance and change, it is not only economic and directly political changes that must be taken into account, and which do not fit our traditional notions. In the vast areas which for so long have been subject to colonial and semi-colonial domination by the imperialist powers, the revival of Islam in a variety of forms has often provided a focus for opposition to 'the West', creating grave problems for the western powers but also for all who seek to take forward a real internationalism. Imperialism's destruction of existing social relations and institutions created a political and cultural wilderness, in which there seemed none but a religion-based opposition to grinding poverty and super-exploitation. It should not come as any surprise that many thousands of young people came forward willing to give their lives for what they see as a holy cause. (And here again it must be emphasised that the traditional leaderships of the working class, social-democratic as well as Stalinist, bear responsibility for the fact that the multi-millioned masses of Asia and Africa have seen the West as the enemy, socially undifferentiated.)

But in the first months of 2011 the people of Tunisia, then Egypt, and soon the whole of North Africa and the Middle East rose up against the exploitation and oppression of their rulers. These rulers were brutal dictatorships sustained and armed by the 'great powers' of the United States, Britain and Western Europe, seeking to defend their interests in oil and 'stability', first against 'communism', then against 'terror'. We all knew that 'a single spark can start a prairie fire', but no one could have predicted that the self-immolation of a young man (not an Islamist suicide bomber but a man fighting for his democratic rights) in Tunis could set alight the whole region? Time and again young people who had joined the movement to overthrow Mubarak proclaimed, 'Neither the military nor the mosque will steal our revolution from us!'

Their confidence will of course be justified only if they find new and strong forms of organisation as well as allies in the neighbouring countries, as well as internationally, to resist the forces of counter-revolution and European/US intervention. But there is an entirely new factor which greatly enhances their prospects. *The spread of he revolution in North Africa and the Middle East was powered by electronic communication, the internet, 'social networking'.* The globalised capital system has been able to expand and intensify its control through the use of these means of communication in production, marketing and the media, but the popular masses in North Africa and the Middle East have shown dramatically in practice what has been potential for some two decades, that these weapons can and will be turned into weapons of resistance and revolution, and this has untold implications for the class struggles of the future, implications to which we return in later sections of this book.

(e) The structural crisis of capital and the class struggle

In the last quarter of the twentieth century a great change took place in the 'advanced' countries. Social-democratic reformism ceased to be an option, and those parties soon became in no real sense working-class parties. In 1989-90 the Soviet Union and Stalinism collapsed under the weight of their contradictions. In effect, the working class was now disenfranchised, and has as yet no political representation or independent political identity, yet it must be recognised as potentially positive for the struggles to come that capital has lost its political agencies for control over the working class.

The twentieth-century political experience surely tells us that the ability of capitalism to take advantage of the absence of internationalism in the organised working-class movement has been for capitalism an enormous advantage, and a disaster for the working class, indeed for the people of all countries (it is surely hardly necessary to mention two world wars). As we have seen, the stage now reached by globalisation means great changes in the relations between the working classes of different countries (the shift of manufacturing to China, the 'mass consumer market' in Europe, the US and Japan, etc), and between the working class and the masses of people in Asia, Africa and Latin America. Clearly then, internationalism, an absolutely central element for the solution of our problem of 'agency', will have to be re-thought, fought for and achieved in a situation very different indeed from that in which it was lost, and fought for, in the nineteenth and twentieth centuries. Here, as we have begun to see, the revolutionised means of communication of the last 20 years can be a highly positive factor.

From the point of view of the ruling class and its apologists, the end of reformism (and Stalinism) marked the victory of capitalism over 'socialism'. Under this illusion they embraced enthusiastically the dogma of privatisation, 'monetarism', 'neo-liberalism', the 'free market', propounded by Hayek, Friedman and their followers. 'Thatcherism'('there is no alternative') and 'Reaganomics' were to provide an economic and political regime which would comfortably contain any threat from the working class. In Britain, for example, the ruling class confidently set about destroying trade unionism in the printing industry, enacting anti-union laws, and 'seeing off the miners' (Thatcher).

What was the reality of this new means of social control, which replaced the Keynesian-type reformism that had served capitalism so well? In the first place, all the talk of liberating the economy and society from the state was lies. In addition to its repressive anti-working-class measures and attack on past hard-won reform gains, the state machine in every country was an indispensable economic support to bankers and multinational companies.

But even this is only the surface of this new reality. The 'globalisation' of which this change was a part intensified the unevenness of the world economy and its internal (economic and national/political) conflicts, rather than being some panacea which would smooth out differences. Secondly, the more globalisation developed, the more any geographical or spatial opportunities for 'exporting' or displacing capital's contradictions disappeared. And finally, to repeat, the death of Stalinism and social-democracy was the end of what had been capital's principal guarantee against any possibility of working-class opposition becoming a challenge to the future of the system.

This reality, in appearance the triumph of free market capitalism, certainly did mark a new phase in capitalism's development, but this new phase, being articulated at an increasing tempo from the 1970s onwards, was in fact capital's structural crisis, within which there would be from time to time 'conjunctural' crises. The economic crisis of 2008-9 was one of these; its severity, duration and aftermath may well tell us that it is not just 'another one' of those conjunctural crises which have always been 'normal' for capitalism, including in its phase of structural crisis, but rather the first of a series of explosions which mark the violent end of that 30 or 40 years of the reign of the free market which succeeded the economic and political mechanisms of capital's so-called 'golden age' following the Second World War and the earlier inter-war periods when the capital system was able in Britain and other countries to restrain working-class opposition through reform concessions. After the Reagan-Thatcher regimes used the state machine to engineer the rapid turn to 'neoliberalism' and the 'free market' the global economy saw nearly 40 years of a feast of speculative movements of 'fictitious capital', the inevitable result of a turn to monetarism under conditions where finance capital had become more dominant than ever before. The financial collapse of 2008-9 was the noisy end of the party.

Can we summarise the implications for the class struggle? No return to social-democratic reformism is possible – indeed, the reforms won in the past are under constant attack. Stalinism is no more. And so the social and political resistance to growing mass unemployment, declining standards of living, destruction of social services, attacks on pensions affecting greater and greater numbers, and so on, cannot be diverted or controlled in the old ways through which the working class could be 'accommodated' and revolutionary movements and outbreaks betrayed as in the twentieth century. We thus confront a question to which as yet there is no answer: after reformism (Keynes, etc) and Stalinism (and in some cases fascism and world war), and after the monetarist bonanza, what next?

Furthermore, the social, economic and political impact of the growth of China's capitalist economy on the old 'advanced' countries, including the strongest of these, the US and Japan, will greatly intensify this problem. The ruling class in China has the undoubted advantage (at least for the period immediately ahead) of the totalitarian system of political-social control over the working population which they brought with them in the course of their seamless transition from state and party Maoist bureaucrats to new capitalist class.

It is surely not at all a mere coincidence that in the middle of this new stage (2008-9 and onwards) of the structural crisis comes the greatly increased tempo and wider and wider recognition of the urgency of the so-called 'ecological crisis'. This ecological threat, it should be re-emphasised here, is the direct consequence of the increasingly ruthless plunder of the planet's resources, the totally unplanned industrial and commercial 'growth' by globalised capital, particularly in its monetarist, free market phase, a growth with no consideration whatsoever of the consequences to nature. How many years ago did István Mészáros and others insist on 'the necessity of social control'?![6] It is this necessity that now imperiously demands recognition and action. Not a 'joint crisis' of economy and ecology, but the fateful progress of capital's structural crisis, a crisis which, no matter what temporary postponements and displacements of the system's contradictions are found, can be overcome only when the system itself is overcome. And here we are inexorably brought back to the central question, that of agency for the necessary structural change, a revolution in our whole way of living.

---

[6] Mészáros, *The Necessity of Social Control*, Merlin Press, 1971.

(f) Agency: the issues

It is a question that will be posed and answered only in an arbitrary and idealist way if our approach to it is not derived from and anchored in the actually existing and developing social-economic-political conditions. Those conditions present us with a series of problems, some of them new, which have to be attacked and their interrelations analysed, before we can begin to make any sense of the 'agency' problem. At various points in the chapters which follow, I attempt to pose these problems as sharply as possible and to outline their significance for the necessary discussion and social practice:

What is the relationship today between the working class, traditionally seen as the agent of socialist revolution, and other social forces?

What are the divisions and differentiations in the working class of, for example, Britain? How have they changed, and what is their significance for the problem of agency?

What is the relation between the working class in the older capitalist countries and the vast majority of today's wage-workers in the emerging capitalist (China etc) countries and 'underdeveloped' countries? Are their interests not mutually opposed? What is the significance of the fact that the workers of the 'advanced capitalist countries', fewer and fewer of them employed in manufacturing, are a necessary 'mass consumer market' for businesses which employ cheap labour in Asia?

What is the significance for the working class, and also for capital, of the existence in the 'overdeveloped countries' of a growing number of permanently (structurally) unemployed and those depending on state benefits, 'proletarians' only in the sense of being propertyless and impoverished? Can they be classed as part of the 'structural antagonist' of capital, the working class? Or are their interests distinct from, even opposed to, those of the employed? What will be their political significance? Will not the existence of this large so-called 'underclass' pose new problems for the building of a new social order?

Is it any longer true (in the older capitalist countries) that the workers 'have nothing to lose but their chains'? Is not the worker's 'subsistence' (the basis of the wage paid to him by his employer) now something very different from the cost of his and his family's daily bread? Clearly, the role of the state, and even of the perceived 'national interest', in relation to the working class, as well as to the banks and capital as a whole, has greatly changed.

How do we critically evaluate and in our changed historical situation go forward from earlier notions of 'socialist consciousness' and 'class-consciousness'? Is it not necessary to understand that, notwithstanding the essential role of theoretical understanding, we must think in terms of consciousness as a process of developing practical consciousness and not a set of answers in the hands of some self-appointed 'leadership'? And must it not be a practical consciousness which already begins to embody the values of the future society, not just the necessity of political revolution?

The latter involves facing up to and understanding the bankruptcy of traditional political forms and the decimation of the trade union movement, now locked into the institutions and ideology of the existing system.

What is the relation of the class interests and movement of the working class to new forms of mobilisation, protest and resistance on the many issues arising from our historical crisis (defence of the natural and built environments, etc)?

What are the realistic prospects of what some writers advocate as making inroads into the capitalist ordering of society even before or in the course of any conquest of state power?

By what means is it possible to begin to establish spatial (networked) and temporal continuity between the many and varied forms of mobilisation against the issues raised by the crisis of capital?

How is it possible to go beyond the theory and practice of those who think it enough to pose the interests of 'civil society' against the state? Surely it is not possible to make viable the 'reclaiming of public space' (let alone 'reclaiming the state', etc), when the prevailing social conditions are structurally based on inequality and domination. Unless these very conditions are overturned, then will not such movements end in an adaptation to the status quo?

Returning to (a) above, we are faced with the question of democracy and freedom. The record of Stalinism and social-democracy has erased from socialism/communism the central and indispensable condition for the society to be achieved through what we have called 'the human revolution'. No renewal of the movement for socialism will be worthy of the name unless freedom is restored to its proper place in theory and practice.

Chapter 2
'Overdeveloped' Countries

(a) Two sides to overdevelopment

Central to the whole question of how, and by what agency, can our future be protected is an understanding of the situation in the 'advanced' capitalist countries as one of overdevelopment. This overdevelopment is a unity of opposites. One side of this contradictory unity is that the material conditions for a socialist future created by the development of productive forces under capitalism, and their implications for human life, have advanced and are advancing beyond the capacity of capital to contain and utilise them in ways which contribute to human fulfilment. Rather, they are more and more perverted, wasteful and destructive. Thus the conquests of science and the promise of abundance, freedom and truly universal intercourse are entrapped. The resources of science and technology are devoted not to the satisfaction of human needs, but solely to inventing and developing ways of accumulating profit, whatever the results in massive waste and destruction of cultural and natural values, because of the grip of capital.

The other side of this overdevelopment is an overdevelopment of capital itself. It is more than a century since Rudolf Hilferding pointed to the growing power of finance-capital in capitalist economy, which he identified with a 'merging' of financial and industrial capital. In point of fact the extent of this 'merging' was very varied in different countries, but the increasing power of finance-capital to which Hilferding pointed has now reached new and gigantic proportions, and it is in the financial sector that globalisation is most developed, thus enhancing its dominance.

This ever-growing power of finance capital in the global arena has rapidly intensified a major contradiction of globalisation, namely, the absence of any political entity corresponding to the economy. Economic measures by national governments become little more than frantic attempts to adjust their budgets to uncontrollable powers and movements in the world's financial markets. In the year 2010 the Eurozone and the wished-for 'monetary union' were laid prostrate for this very reason. Finance capital's dominance has greatly accelerated, especially since the Reagan-Thatcher monetarist, 'neo-liberal' (actually, writes François Chesnais, neo-conservative) deregulation of financial markets (it is by no means insignificant that these changes were contemporaneous with Deng Xiao-ping's 1980 reforms in China). In the last 30 years the economy has become subject to the trading on a massive scale of investment and speculation in capital funds which are in no way destined ever to enter the cycle of production, yet must claim a return. Debts are traded, often scores of times each, on the expectation of future profits. Profits can of course in the last analysis only be a share of the total value of products, yet a return is demanded on capital which never enters production. The financial chaos of 2007-9 resulting from this kind of trading necessitated state intervention to rescue banks and slow down the consequent 'recession'. The immediate cause of this last crisis was the 'sub-prime' market. Until the early 1990s, mortgages for house purchase in the US and Britain were offered only to those with a degree of financial security and/or in full-time work. Then 'sub-prime' mortgages became available to high-risk borrowers. The debts incurred were then traded on a massive scale. These so-called securities were literally fictitious capital.

The consequences of the 2007-9 crisis are there for all to see: slowing down of productive investment, increase in unemployment, sweeping cuts in social welfare and essential services. These result not only from the decisions of company investors but, more decisively, from the measures taken by governments who find their countries' exchange-rates and indebtedness moving in directions which inevitably respond to the global changes resulting from the global financial markets. Britain, with its over-reliance on the City of London, was not the only country whose government was obliged to take such measures. France sees a rapid decline in social services, and Greece was forced almost to the point of bankruptcy, with Spain and Portugal not far behind.

These experiences were not new, but an intensification of a process already under way. Chesnais writes that the new phase of the dominance of finance-capital, beginning around 1980, and 'the weakness of the working-class movement ... are at the same time cause and consequence of the neo-liberal politics which have deregulated international exchanges of goods, of services, and of capital, privatised public services and attacked state welfare provision since the early 80s.' (It should not be forgotten that, along with the Reagan-Thatcher economic innovations went the offensive to break the power of the trade unions in the US air traffic control strike and in the defeats of miners and printworkers in the UK.) The growing power of financial logic (the use of pension funds, manipulation of financial markets) weighs more and more heavily on industrial businesses and on states/governments. Long ago John Maynard Keynes insisted that 'rentier' capital's interests were incompatible with an economy resting on investment and full employment. The days when Keynesian economics could be the basis of policies for full employment and state welfare systems are long gone, and the triumph of monetarism and rentier capital is the final blow. It was one thing for countries like Mexico and Thailand to feel the impact of the new order in the 1990s, but this now comes to Britain and Western Europe. To this must be added the new problems of the rise of China (and India), where vast amounts of US-, European- and Japanese-based capital have been placed.

To return to our 'overdevelopment as a unity of opposites'. The productive forces and means of communication (which in any case are more and more coinciding) have developed to a level far, far beyond what could be imagined in the days of Marx, Engels, Lenin and Trotsky ... a level far higher than would then have been considered sufficient material basis for a socialist society and human freedom. It is because these advances coincide with the persistence of capitalism and its imperatives ('accumulation for accumulation's sake'), now overdeveloped in the form of unregulated movements of financial capital, largely fictitious, that we ought now to say that the 'advanced capitalist countries' are overdeveloped countries. The pathological problems of these countries – crime, social and moral breakdown, collapse of norms, etc – are basically the result of the entrapment of these highly developed productive forces in the process of reproduction of capital, its 'destructive self-reproduction' (Mészáros).

So perhaps each of the component parts of what follows in this book can be seen as aspects of this overdevelopment, this entrapment, and the problems it poses. The same framework is consistent with the emphasis I laid in *Not Without a Storm* (Index Books, 2006) on defending, protecting and developing the basic premises of a future socialist society. 'Develop' should here be understood in the sense of 'try to find ways of developing these cultural and natural foundations in a way which opposes the mode and purposes of their development by capital, frees them from their entrapment in capital's imperatives and the evil agencies spawned by capital's over-lasting rule'.

(b) Overdevelopment and 'underdevelopment'

Marx's emphasis on the proletarian revolution being 'the human revolution', and not a revolution that replaces one class's domination with another, is totally consistent with the understanding that this overdevelopment, so long as it is entrapped, undermines, even destroys, the precious human content which we need to make the revolution. This recalls Vasily Grossman's sifting basic acts of human kindness out of the bloody conflict of the Second World War (in his novel *Life and Fate*). This aspect of overdevelopment is no doubt more difficult to understand and explain than the 'overdevelopment' of exploitation of nature and its resources, but it is equally decisive for the understanding of our situation and our tasks.

The overdeveloped countries are inextricably part of the global economy, so that the continued, indeed worsening, so-called underdevelopment of countries in Asia, Africa and Latin America (as well as the deformed development of the 'emerging economies') is organically linked to Europe's and North America's overdevelopment. The rise of capitalism in Britain, Western Europe and North America depended to a very great extent on colonialism and neo-colonialism, on the imperialist plunder of the colonial countries' resources, and on the exploitation of their labour (including slave labour), and today it is giant transnational corporations based in the overdeveloped countries that ruthlessly exploit the 'underdeveloped' nations.

Summarising: the 'underdevelopment' of Asian, African and Latin American countries is the product and the other side of the development, and now the overdevelopment, of the countries of Western Europe and North America. As István Mészáros put it: the maintenance of '"advanced" capital's highly stretched and absurdly "overdeveloped" system of production ... necessarily postulates the continued domination of a vast "hinterland" of enforced underdevelopment.' And this necessity is the other side of an insoluble contradiction, as capital in its 'globalised' stage '... must at the same time propel the "Third World" to a high level of capitalistic development (which could only reproduce the contradictions of western "advanced" capital, multiplied by the immense size of the population involved).'[7]

(c) Changes in the working class

The fact that at the beginning of the twenty-first century we find ourselves more than 40 years beyond the onset of the capital system's structural crisis (in the 1970s), with the capitalist countries of Europe and North America now 'overdeveloped' (in the sense explained above of the contradiction between socialised production and the exploitation of wage-labour), demands a radical rethinking of many of our twentieth-century ideas on socialist revolution.

Some examples:

For many years it was of great importance (in opposition to the Stalinist 'socialism in a single country') to understand Lenin's insistence, following the Russian revolution of October 1917, that only when proletarian revolution succeeded in the 'advanced capitalist countries' could the Soviet Union hope to survive and make the transition to socialism. Clearly this no longer suffices: the Soviet Union is no more, there was no successful revolution in the advanced countries, and the relation between the latter and the

---

[7] Mészáros, *Beyond Capital*, Monthly Review Press, 1995, p. 693

rest of the world has changed, with the great majority of proletarians now outside Europe and North America, many of them employed by transnational corporations, directly or indirectly.

Communists fought for a 'united front' of working-class parties, but today the parties of social-democracy, reformism (Labour Party, etc) are no longer working-class parties in any sense.

Trotsky based his 'Transitional Programme' on the idea that 'mankind's productive forces stagnate', but they have since undergone an unprecedented development.

Communists followed Lenin in seeing twentieth-century imperialism as 'the highest stage of capitalism' (even often misunderstanding it as the last stage); it was, but is no longer. And so on.

To understand the situation in the 'advanced capitalist countries' as one of 'overdevelopment' poses new problems. Take the question of unemployment. What are the implications of unemployment's now being largely structural rather than conjunctural?

In particular: if unemployed workers were in the past part of the working class (a 'reserve army of labour'), what can be said of the large numbers now who are permanently unemployed? Since most of them are unlikely ever to be working, so that capital does not depend on exploiting them, then how can they be said to be part of that 'structural antagonist' of capital, the working class? They are proletarians only in the sense that they have nothing. As such, they form a growing part of the mass of people proletarianised, dispossessed and disempowered.

They do not depend on wages, they are not fundamental to the social metabolism of the system. On the contrary, they are in an important sense a drain on the system's productive powers. At the same time, their spending power is a necessity for capital's ability to 'realise' the value of its products in the 'mass consumer market'.

The economic relationship between employed workers and those dependent on state benefits, and between each of them and the state, is a highly complex one. In the first place, as a result of past reformist gains, employed workers and their families, as well as unemployed, retired and disabled people are heavily dependent on state-financed services, utilities and welfare benefits. One-third of all families in Britain in 2010 depended on state benefits for more than 50 per cent of their income! Education, health services and the whole infrastructure of daily life depend on the state budget. This same infrastructure is also, of course, indispensable to capital, to every business (despite the propaganda claptrap about a 'free market economy' and non-dependence on the state). But how is the state itself financed, if not, in large part, by taxing the income of workers? Wages, payment for the worker's labour-time to meet his subsistence needs, must include enough for him or her to pay these taxes. Employers also pay taxes, but where does the means to pay their taxes come from, if not from the value produced by their workers and appropriated as profit? Thus, when workers produce, they produce enough not only to feed the employer with profit but also to fill the coffers of the state, which must distribute benefits to the population, including the non-employed. (For present purposes, I ignore other state expenditures – 'defence', etc, – which obviously are similarly financed.)

It is thus an oversimplification, in this day and age, to see the wage of a worker in simple terms of elementary subsistence (even when acknowledging that subsistence is a historically changing entity as living standards improve), a wage to be fought over only by workers in their unions ('combinations') against individual employers. Undoubtedly much class conflict will continue initially to take the form of action against employers in defence of wages and jobs, as the basic defence against increased cost of living, sackings and so on. But the conditions of workers (and not only of workers) clearly now depend on a massive structure of state revenues and expenditures, and on the effects on these of global economic forces.

There is no avoiding the fact that resistance to attacks and threats to employment and living standards must more and more come to take on a political character, that is, the character of conflicts at the level of government, of the state power. Exactly what kinds of social and political action and organisation this will necessitate is not known in advance and not a matter for speculation. The only way forward is to study and engage with all forms of resistance and protest, understanding that many of these will not begin as in any way explicitly socialist, and will often involve sections of society other than the working class. Reverting to our discussion of the position of permanently unemployed and others dependent entirely on state benefits, we must expect them to find the need for forms of rebellion and protest as well as their being conditioned to acqiescence and apathy.

The relationship between the mass, on every continent, of propertyless and impoverished people, and in that sense proletarians, and the employed or potentially employed working class, is a matter of first-class importance for the struggle to overcome capitalism, along with that of the relations which need to be secured between the working class and its potential allies (peasantry, intellectuals).[8] At worst, if this question remains unsolved, we run the risk of repeating the long history of impoverished workers being used against the working class, a history certainly not finished. For example, as recently as 1976-7 it was the dispossessed of the kibeles in Addis Ababa who physically carried out the 'red terror' against the left and the trade unions at the instigation of the Dergue. And in the same category is the recent 'ethnic cleansing' in Rwanda and in the Balkans. For the working-class movement and its necessary reorientation, it is surely imperative that the youth and unemployed of the rotting urban areas of the big cities and the once-industrial wastelands are not left to their own devices, to rebel against their virtual ghettoisation and be brutally suppressed. Instead of the often-heard bleatings like 'these riots are pointless' or 'these rebellious youth cannot succeed without coming to the side of the working class', socialists will need to fight for working-class organisations to support, against state repression, those who rebel, like the youth of Paris denounced as scum by Nicolas Sarkozy.

---

[8] Henri Lefebvre wrote of '... an immense proletarianisation alongside the working class itself, together with new conflictive elements. If one defines the proletariat by its lack of practical juridical links with he means of production, then proletarianisation affects everyone – the middle classes, white-collar workers, landless peasants who (in Latin America, for example) are not integrated into production, and the urban peripheries in general. This vast proletarianisation of the world contrasts with the working-class bloc, which stays solid. It includes youth, and intellectuals whom learning fails to link with the means of production; it includes blacks and immigrant workers. It is an enormous process, corresponding with the utmost precision to the initial Marxist notion of a class separated from the means of production, charged with negativity, and capable under certain conditions of a struggle to the death to change everything.' (*The Survival of Capitalism*, Allison & Busby, 1976, p. 97)

However, it is interesting here to consider an overlooked side of the well-known decline of manufacturing and new predominance of the 'service sector'. The traditional form of strike struggles and their culmination in general strikes depended on the organisation of workers in manufacturing industry. There is an apparent problem for service workers in planning strike action. In many, many cases (public health, education, social welfare provision, etc), such strikes are not threats directed at a capitalist employer or group of employers; their immediate effect is to endanger the conditions of those 'served' by these services. What is needed is united organisation and action, on the basis of common interest, of those working in and those served by the service sector. This has suddenly become an urgent question, as resistance builds up against the savage cuts in all public services, the killing off of the 'welfare state', the 'third-worldisation' of the advanced countries of Europe and America.

This continuous attack, in the form of budgetary cuts, hits millions dependent on social services, and hardest of all the unemployed. It will politicise millions who have not been engaged politically in any way and will resist the cuts. That resistance is obviously directly connected to the resistance of workers in the services. Even more important, its demands are directly political, not simply economic, directed at employers. Its form, already manifest, is the mass street demonstration (compare the movements in North Africa and the Middle East). What is posed is the great question of how such movements can be organised, united, in such a way as to assure their spatial and temporal continuity. This goes beyond trade unionism (though as it builds up into a mass struggle against the state, it will involve trade unions and strikes), and beyond parliamentary politics. It demands new forms of mass self-organisation. It has revolutionary implications.

By the last years of the twentieth century, the working-class movement had been decimated. Trade unions still exist, but they organise a much smaller proportion of the working class, and they are in many cases reduced to the level of bureaucratised service agencies (legal advice and protection for individual members, etc), having abandoned any sort of opposition to capital as the ruling power. The reformist parties (Labour, social-democrat) no longer represent the social, let alone the political, interests of the working class. They accept the capitalist system as permanent, as in Thatcher's 'There is no alternative'. The Communist Parties have collapsed with the disintegration of the Stalinist regimes in the Soviet Union, Eastern Europe and China. Long before that, they had abandoned any independent working-class politics in favour of 'peaceful coexistence with capitalism' and the myth of 'peaceful, parliamentary roads to socialism'. And, very important for this present project, Stalinism thoroughly undermined and in most cases completely destroyed all optimism for socialist progress, so that today it is hard to imagine any possibility of movements of young people aspiring to a socialist society.

The collapse of the traditional socialist and communist movements opened the door wider to the dominance of individualism, self-seeking and 'consumerism'. These were always pervasive in capitalist society, but they now predominate more and more, given full rein by the characteristics of what I am calling the 'overdevelopment' of the older capitalist countries. I will try to expand on this statement. In his early work, *The Condition of the Working Class in England in 1844*, Engels wrote of:

> The brutal indifference, the unfeeling isolation of each in his private interest ... this narrow self-seeking is the fundamental principle of our society everywhere... Hence it comes, too, that the social war, the war of each against all, is here openly declared.

In 1844, the poverty inflicted on the working class led to

> ... those who have not yet sunk in the whirlpool of moral ruin which surrounds them, sinking daily deeper, losing daily more and more of their power to resist the demoralising influence of want, filth, and evil surroundings.

Thus the demoralisation, the crime, the 'intemperances' of the 1840s were put down to poverty, a poverty which was to a great extent reduced and in some cases eliminated, by the concessions and reforms which the ruling class was able to afford in the face of working-class organisation over a century and more.

Even though the return of poverty and deprivation on a growing scale is very visible, and the exhaustion of the possibility of significant reforms is every day more evident, it is not possible to attribute today's rampant self-seeking, decline of social solidarity, increasing crime rate and so on, to the same immediate causes. The self-seeking individualism seen by Engels as the 'fundamental principle' of the society serving capital remains just that, but it now takes malignant forms resulting from the rotten-ripeness of capitalism, the entrapment of highly developed productive forces and human capacities in capitalist social relations. The absolutely unprecedented growth of productivity, especially with information technology, while opening up the possibility of future abundance and truly human freedom, is today instead the basis for at best a tawdry consumerism and a brutal individualism.

This 'overdevelopment' is at the root of 'the condition of the working class in England in 2009'. It raises new and very difficult problems for the development of what the young Marx called the 'mass communist consciousness' necessary for the transition to socialism, and even for the elementary working-class solidarity which he saw in the early English trade unions. Today, in Britain and the United States for example, less than 20 per cent of employed people work in factories and workshops, traditionally the focus of trade union organisation and solidarity. But equally important is the fact that people's consciousness is concentrated on individual interests dominated by the massive and invasive market in consumer goods which go far beyond mere subsistence. Individualism and self-seeking are the opposite of solidarity and mutual aid.

Furthermore, this condition is compounded by the reality that increasingly the countries of Western Europe, Britain and the US become the mass consumer market counterpart of the mass production (using cheap labour) of goods in China, India and SE Asia. Certainly this mass of consumers is 'necessary' to, say, British capitalism, but not at all in the same way as is the working class as producers, selling their labour-power. Indeed, rather than having the opposed interests of a 'structural antagonist', they can in a certain sense be said to have a common interest with the employing class in enjoying some of the fruits of Asian cheap labour.

On the other hand, in the case of Britain, gross overdependence of the national economy on the financial sector (the City of London) exposes it to massive indebtedness and other problems which are making necessary sweeping cuts in infrastructure, essential services (health, education) and welfare, as well as in salaries, pensions and jobs. These, part of what Mészáros has called 'the downward equalisation of the rate of exploitation', will inevitably provoke protest and resistance which, if they are to succeed, will have to be armed with a new consciousness and new forms of organisation. And if these defensive battles are to be transformed into the necessary strategic offensive, they will need to develop international perspectives and organised international connections.

Clearly, in the light of the gigantic changes consequent on the globalisation of capital and the unprecedented development of the means of production and communication, it is imperative that we do all we can to develop our ideas beyond those with which we and our forebears responded to the conditions of the twentieth and nineteenth centuries. The most important question to be addressed, as we have seen, is that of agency, i.e. the question of who will carry out the overcoming of capital's rule, and how. Marxists hold, above all else, that the structural antagonist of capital is the working class. The international solidarity of this class was always a necessity, but the relationship between its national components has radically changed (a change superadded to the greatly changed internal and occupational structure of the class).

Is Britain (or the United States or Western Europe, for that matter) still 'the workshop of the world'? Surely not. It is decades since Germany became the world's biggest exporter of manufactured goods, only to be overtaken by China in January 2010.

China and India now contain the majority of the world's wage-workers. These workers come into the class struggle against capital in ways very different from those taken by the working class of Marx's day, or of our own twentieth-century experience. In China, they are fighting to organise in the factories owned by transnational corporations and by the new-born native capitalists who in most cases retain their offices in the bureaucratic state machine inherited from the collapsed Stalinist 'socialism' (perhaps we should call China 'the sweatshop of the world'?). But there are thousands of protest movements all over China on issues which bring workers and peasants into confrontation with the authorities – the demands for democratic rights exemplified by Tiananmen Square, the fight against the seizure of land by bureaucrats/capitalists for 'development', against the scandals of housing and urban planning, against the mass unemployment of 'migrant' workers as the world slump of 2008-9 begins to bite. More and more these movements have begun to organise themselves into networks which establish spatial and temporal continuity. And it is computers and the internet which make this coordination possible. Similar movements on social issues are taking place in Russia, where the lead is taken in most cases by younger people, and in particular by women in their thirties. Because of the particular mode of formation of the new capitalist class emerging from Stalinism in these countries, the struggles there bring workers into direct conflict with the state, that is to say politically, and not only with particular employers.

Lenin told his comrades after the October revolution that Russia would remain too backward and isolated for the building of socialism 'until the workers of the advanced capitalist countries come to our aid'. Will our prospects in the now overdeveloped countries perhaps soon be improved as 'the workers of the new capitalist countries come to our aid'?

Chapter 3
Overdevelopment has social-pathological results

(a) Overdevelopment and the condition of the working class

Capital's 'overdevelopment' has social aspects which create further divisions and internal contradictions within the proletariat. In the older capitalist countries, past concessions won by the organisations of the working class, and necessary to the ruling class as concessions to stave off opposition (the 'welfare state', etc.), have left in place the institutions and policies that allow millions to exist on benefits, even creating a whole culture of 'working the system'. Many of these men and women, it goes without saying, have real needs which they cannot meet in any other way. Society does not offer them the means to live a dignified life. The alienation inherent in capitalist exploitation is here greatly accentuated. These millions are parasitic on the social body (using the word parasitic without any moral judgment whatsoever). Nonetheless, their relation to the rest of the working class is not a fixed one. More and more, following the financial and debt crisis of 2008-9, the governments of the overdeveloped capitalist countries are compelled to attack the 'welfare state' (the 'benefits culture', as they call it), making life near-impossible for millions. The result will be to rouse from political apathy large numbers of men and women, as their interests come into direct conflict with the state. What the character of their politics will be – it could be radically progressive but it could be reactionary, used against the working class if there is no socialist alternative which can find ways of addressing people's real needs –

we do not yet know. The conflict will soon be exacerbated as the workers of China and India begin to succeed in winning wage increases, thus affecting the supply of cheap imported goods in Europe and America.

Those who live primarily by small-scale trading, 'fiddling', exploiting the spending power of others, at a level where criminal (and worse, destructive of human beings, drugs being the prime example), semi-criminal, fraudulent aspects are common, are also parasitic, in a different way, namely: in the older capitalist countries, the same needs of capital which allowed the growth of the welfare state have resulted in the existence of a working class which lives above the bare subsistence wage-level of the nineteenth century. Capitalism today is more parasitic than ever, much of capitalist 'enterprise' being devoted not to production of use-values but to getting back from consumers the money they have earned. Can it not be argued that the rampant 'subcultures' of illicit dealing – especially drugs, confidence-trickery, 'scams' – are a parasitic feeding off this availability of money for consumers, 'punters'? It involves, often, the employment for wages ('on the black') of other men and women, but the activity of such workers is not productive, not fundamental or necessary to the capitalist social system.

Thus far, we have considered only the basic socio-economic nature of a social group, the 'structurally unemployed', asking: in what sense can they be called part of the working class as 'structural antagonist' of capital? There are, however, very important political, ideological, moral aspects. Even at a directly observable level, the reduction of millions of people to dependence on drugs is a basic reality on which the dealers feed. And so the question is immediately posed: why this mass dependence on drugs? Why are there large numbers of people prepared or persuaded to engage in the inhuman activities involved in such a trade? (It should of course not be forgotten that every person driven to drug-addiction and every small drug-dealer is at the bottom rung of a commercial ladder which reaches to millionaire bosses.) It is surely the same question as: how could the recent (2008-9) spate of stabbings and shootings, especially involving young people, come about? How can we explain the apparently growing readiness of young men to kill, in this day and age? The powers that be and their self-serving agencies and apologists can do no more than condemn those driven to criminal and 'anti-social' behaviour, and every day look for new ways of meting out punishment or 'rehabilitation'. But the problem cannot be dealt with at the level of individual motivation and reform. It is a social problem, a pathological symptom of a sickness of the social system, its overdevelopment.

These symptoms are the products of capitalist society's oppression, its criminality, its infliction of alienation. Like the revolt of youth in 2005 in the poor quarters of Paris, characterised by politicians and the media as 'riots' of those called 'scum' by Nicolas Sarkozy, they are the effects, not the causes, of social breakdown. When the place where people live becomes a prison, everything inherent in places of incarceration develops: violence, humiliation of everyone, victimisation of the weaker by the stronger. Point the finger not at individuals who commit crime, but at the society whose metabolism is regulated by capital and its imperatives. In the same sense, it would surely be wrong to try to explain the rate of crime in terms of individual motivation and behaviour. In the United Sates, for example, over two million people are in prison. Fifty per cent of these prisoners are black. The figures have more than doubled in the last 20 years. Every year more prisons are privatised.

What we have here is a manifestation of the reality that the fundamental contradiction – between socialised production on the one hand and the continuation of capital's inherent need to reproduce and enhance itself by the 'theft of alienated labour time' on the other – has become unbearably destructive, not only to external nature but also to humanity and our cultural heritage. As we have seen, capital must always confine the new 'giant social forces' and their productive power within the limits of the search for surplus value – at whatever cost to humanity.

(b) Overdeveloped capital is criminal – some examples

Archaeology, now enriched by the achievements of physics, chemistry and genetics, can more than ever reveal to us the truth of human origins and past civilisations, but capital's 'security' in 2004 in Iraq required the destruction of the heritage of Mesopotamian civilisation.

And in 2005 George W. Bush and all the 'personifications of capital' in the US could not 'afford' to save New Orleans and its people, the creators of the wonders of jazz music. Millions have seen a video of Bush, being shown in advance in graphic terms what was in danger of happening to New Orleans – advice which he totally ignored. This man and those behind him justify their murderous 'war on terror' by promising to defend American interests and security. Whose security, then? Whose interests? American 'culture' at this point brought billions of dollars profit for investors in the aftermath of the disaster, and in that aftermath a reduction of many of the poorest people in New Orleans to a virtually Hobbesian condition of 'war of each against all', a life 'nasty, brutish and short'.

Some people did not see the destruction wrought by Hurricane Katrina as by any means an unmitigated disaster. The following examples are taken from Naomi Klein's incomparable *The Shock Doctrine* (2007), about what she calls 'disaster capitalism'. Republican Congressman Richard Baker declared: 'We finally cleaned up public housing in New Orleans. We couldn't do it, but God did.' And Joseph Canizoro, one of New Orleans' wealthiest property developers, saw his way to 'clean up': 'I think we have a clean sheet to start again. And with that clean sheet we have some very big opportunities.'(p. 4)

Another seeker after opportunities, Milton Friedman, economist and high priest of monetarism, inspirer of Reagan and Thatcher, wrote in the *Wall Street Journal*: 'Most New Orleans schools are in ruins, as are the homes of the children who attended them. The children are now scattered all over the country. This is a tragedy. It is also an opportunity to radically reform the educational system.'(Ibid, pp. 4-5.) 'Radical' meant using millions from the available disaster relief funds to provide vouchers to parents, for use in sending their children to schools run by private entrepreneurs for profit ('charter schools'). Before Katrina, New Orleans had 123 public (i.e. non-private) schools. Now there are four. And 4,700 unionised teachers have been sacked.

It goes without saying that such are not the views of many New Orleans citizens. Again, from Naomi Klein:

Over at the shelter, Jamar could think of nothing else. 'I really don't see it as cleaning up the city. What I see is that a lot of people got killed uptown. People who shouldn't have died.'

He was speaking quietly, but an older man in line in front of us overheard and whipped around. 'What is wrong with these people in Baton Rouge? This isn't an opportunity. It's a goddamned tragedy. Are they blind?' A mother with two kids chimed in. 'No, they're not blind, they're evil. They see just fine.' (Ibid, p. 4)

This mother was surely right, saying in her own direct way what has been known by the 'lower orders' for centuries about the way to understand crime. It is not enough for radical criminologists to show only that today's society is 'criminogenic' – the society itself is a crime. It is guilty of fraud, criminal damage, grievous bodily harm, theft, mass murder and many other offences. A good first lesson for criminologists was laid down centuries ago by rural workers hit by the English Enclosures:

> The law locks up the man or woman
> Who steals the goose from off the common,
> But leaves the greater villain loose,
> Who steals the common from the goose

Much later, across the Atlantic, Woody Guthrie and Pete Seeger sang the cowboy song 'Pretty Boy Floyd':

> Now gather round me children
> And a story I will tell,
> About Pretty Boy Floyd an outlaw,
> Oklahoma knew him well.
> It was in the town of Shawnee,
> It was Saturday afternoon,
> His wife beside him in his carriage,
> As in the town they rode.
> Now the deputy sheriff approached them,
> In a manner rather rude,

Using vulgar words and language
And his wife she overheard.
Pretty Boy took out his lock and chain,
And the deputy pulled his gun,
And in the fight that followed,
He laid that deputy down.
He fled to the hills and woodlands,
To live a life of shame,
Every crime in Oklahoma,
Was added to his name.
As through this world you wander,
You'll meet lots of funny men
Some will rob you with a six-gun,
And some with a fountain pen.
Now wherever you may wander,
Wherever you may roam,
You will never see an outlaw,
Drive a family from their home.

Yes: families were and are driven from their homes, in the interests of banks, with society's laws legitimising this crime (theft), just as the enclosures drove people off the land, legally, in the era of transition from feudalism to capitalism (a process now being repeated in China). Our own day's globalised capitalism performs crimes even more monstrous, with the instruments available from the massive state resources of great powers.

Here one example will suffice, taken from the long list compiled by Francis Wheen. It concerns the reports of the US Pike Commission, which investigated 'covert intervention by the US in Iran and Iraq during the 1970s':

> The committee members found that in 1972 Henry Kissinger and Richard Nixon had told the Shah of Iran that Iraq was upsetting the 'balance of power' in the Gulf, and that this could best be remedied by exhorting the Kurds in northern Iraq to revolt against the Baathist regime. As the Pike Report revealed: 'Documents in the committee's possession clearly show that the President, Dr Kissinger and the foreign head of

state (the Shah) hoped that our clients (the Kurds) would not prevail. They preferred instead that the insurgents simply continue a level of hostilities sufficient to sap the resources of our ally's neighbouring country (Iraq). This policy was not imparted to our clients, who were encouraged to continue fighting.' But it was imparted to Saddam Hussein, then the deputy leader in Baghdad, who eventually took the hint. He and the Shah signed a treaty in 1975 ending their border dispute and restoring the region's 'balance': on the very same day Washington abruptly cut off aid to the Kurds, and Saddam began his long Blitzkrieg against the Kurdistan.[9]

Here was a crime of mass murder. Kissinger (who was awarded the Nobel Peace Prize for his efforts - hence Tom Lehrer's 'the age of satire is dead'), Reagan and others were certainly criminal. But the point here is that the overdeveloped capital system now requires, for its continued functioning, that such crimes be perpetrated. And for the same reasons, it became necessary only a short time later for Iraq itself to be subjected to destruction.

The destruction of Kurdistan, then of Iraq, was a crime; New Orleans was a crime; and there were and are countless others of the same kind. As though the earlier part of the twentieth century were not enough ... As Vasily Grossman wrote in his masterpiece *Life and Fate*:

> The first half of the twentieth century may be seen as a time of forgotten great scientific discoveries, revolutions, immense social transformations and two world wars. It will go down in history, however, as the time when – in accordance with philosophies of race and society – whole sections of the Jewish population were exterminated. Understandably, the present day remains discreetly silent about this. (Vintage Classics, 2006)

---

[9] Francis Wheen, *How Mumbo Jumbo Conquered the World*, Harper Perennial, 2004. pp. 176-7

(c) Waking from the nightmare

Rosa Luxemburg knew early in the last century that it was to be 'socialism or barbarism'. We got the barbarism of fascism in Germany, Italy, Spain and Japan, Stalinism in the Soviet Union, ethnic extermination in Rwanda and the Balkans, apartheid and colonial wars, two world wars, atomic bombs. And no socialism. That tells us much about the twentieth century. In our own twenty-first century, socialism and barbarism are still the alternatives, but now we have not only barbarism but the undoubted threat of destruction, unless the working class can organise and arm itself to defeat globalised capital. We need to overcome the experience of the twentieth century in more ways than one. One of Walter Benjamin's profound insights in the 1920s was paraphrased by Rolf Tiedemann, in an addendum to Benjamin's *The Arcades Project*: 'The nineteenth century is the dream we must wake up from: it is a nightmare that will weigh on the present as long as its spell remains unbroken.' (Harvard UP, 1999, p. 935)

Surely now we must say the same for our own 'nightmare' of the twentieth century. Waking up from it means 'the genuine liberation from an epoch' (ibid). We have the duty to contribute to the actions, the practice, that will overcome the twentieth century's barbarism of oppression, exploitation and war, which continues into our own millennium. And to equip ourselves we have to overcome the severe limitations of and go beyond the 'dreams' we had of liberation in the last century. That means, we might say, a 'bonfire of the certainties'.

As we have already seen, imperialism and globalisation of capital had social and political consequences in which competition between workers of different countries (especially 'developed' and 'underdeveloped' countries) was added to the ever-present potential divisions of interest within the working class (employed/unemployed, skilled and better-paid/unskilled and poorly paid, settled/immigrant), These, like the 'pathological' effects dealt with above, are great problems not only for the unity and effectiveness of the working class in its struggle to put an end to capitalist rule, but also for the transition period following, in which the working class must liberate itself from the inherited alienating and authoritarian division of labour.

It is clearly not enough for socialists to simply repeat to themselves that only the working class is the structural antagonist of capital, the class that must organise to achieve its own self-emancipation. The internal differentiation and oppositions within the working class amount to a global problem (it is a globally interconnected capital system that must be confronted and overcome) which must be constantly engaged with and overcome in the course of the great struggles which will burst forth as capital encounters the deepening contradictions in its unfolding structural crisis, forcing it to impose the costs on the working class. A mass movement with the potential to challenge capitalist rule will not come into existence so long as the system is able to make concessions which make life bearable. There is no doubt that only in great crises and struggles can there emerge the solidarity, organisation and consciousness necessary to overcome the divisions in the world working class. This should not be taken to mean that such a positive development is an inevitable consequence. Once again it must be stressed that without the recovery and reconstruction on a new basis of the internationalism and solidarity of the working class the field will be open to exploitation of discontent and desperation by reactionary forces, as the history of fascism has shown.

That reconstruction is the central and overriding task confronting socialists. Not a single one of the old forms of union and political-party organisation can be called up to be effective in this task, even though the lessons of past struggles will be indispensable.

We can and must add that the new consciousness of the fateful threat now posed to nature and culture will bring to the side of the working class many, many scientists, artists, writers and other intellectuals. The completely unprecedented advance in information technology has been unbelievably profitable for capital, but its potential as an organiser in the struggle for socialism becomes daily more apparent (Marx and Engels, after all, did not even have a telephone, and Lenin wanted a daily paper as an 'organiser').

To these advantages should be added the positive significance of the death of Stalinism and of Social-Democracy. As always, this is one side of a contradictory development. As capital now has to dispense with reformism, even needing to wrest back past concessions, and with Stalinism gone, the state is quickly becoming less and less a benevolent provider, and its fundamental repressive functions already begin to predominate.

(d) Capital has bolted

A succinct summary of what is written in the last two chapters on 'overdeveloped countries' would be to say, using a phrase from plant cultivation, that capital has 'bolted'.

The dictionary definition is:

Bolt: run to seed
Run to seed: 1.cease flowering as seed develops
Run to seed: 2.become degenerate, unkempt, ineffective, etc.

Chapter 4

Socialisation of production – and communism

(a) The potential of forces of production

The most fundamental theoretical and practical problem facing those who understand the necessity of fundamental social and economic change is to understand in what way the vastly changed economic, social and political reality of today, a century and a half after Marx's mature work, demands a development of his conclusion that the working class was the revolutionary force which would take society beyond the rule of capital, and to find ways to act upon that understanding.

Were not Marx's words prophetic and not merely descriptive of his own day?

> Hence the highest development of productive power together with the greatest expansion of existing wealth will coincide with depreciation of capital, degradation of the labourer, and a most straitened exhaustion of his vital powers.

> The accumulation of knowledge and of skill, of the general productive forces of the social brain, is thus absorbed into capital, as opposed to labour, and hence appears as an attribute of capital, and more specifically of fixed capital, insofar as it enters into the production process as a means of production proper. (*Grundrisse*, Penguin, 1973, p. 694)

And

> The development of fixed capital indicates to what degree general social knowledge has become a direct force of production, and to what degree, hence, the conditions of the process of social life itself have come under the control of the general intellect and been transformed in accordance with it (p. 707).

As well as being essential for understanding the real significance of Information Technology, this last sentence surely points to the necessity of protecting and defending (and furthering?) these 'conditions of the process of social life' – now 'under the control of the general intellect' but with the resources of this 'general intellect' alienated from the direct producers in the hands of capital and standing over and against the labourer.

Here it is surely necessary to consider the implications and significance of the 'information revolution'. Not only are the means of production transformed, but also the composition and conditions of the working class (and remember that the working class is the most important productive force of all). Marx famously wrote that capital produces, and cannot but produce, its own 'gravediggers'- the working class created in the Industrial Revolution, already organising itself in 'combinations', trade unions.

This bears reflection today. Selling computers, having people to operate them, marketing and advertising by means of them, controlling production processes by means of them, managing world-wide financial and commercial mechanisms through them – all these are now absolutely essential to capital. But the internet and email, means of universal communication, are free, and available to millions! Means of communication, they are potentially means of organisation, means of interchange and cross-fertilisation of science and of the lessons of experience, means of the immediate coordination of movements. In this sense, the advantages of what Marx had already called 'the annihilation of space by time'(!) are now available to us too! Clearly, potentially possible now is a collective understanding and mastery of nature, an understanding extending globally, in which individuals are consciously part of the collective and can share in that understanding and mastery. What they do not yet have is the true wealth that has become possible.

Surely the advent of computers, the internet, electronic control of production, communication and media is the ultimate form of what Marx called socialisation of production and the 'social brain'. Referring to the coming of a world market and the means of communication and transport making it possible, Marx wrote of 'the conquest of space by time'. We are now living in a world market a million times more advanced in that respect. Capital needs electronic communication and the media to programme and control people's work, their consumption, their wants and aspirations, their consent, their resting in ignorance of their real condition. Every aspect of this control, in the working of a system now globalised, is necessary for the metabolism of society (of course this does not mean that older methods of control and repression are outdated – on the contrary, they are resorted to whenever necessary).

However, this necessity, for capital, of having all aspects of people's lives 'wired up', means at the same time that there are so many more points at which the system is vulnerable to disruption, just as the interconnected world-wide operations of transnational companies makes them more vulnerable to workers' action. Already in the 1990s this was becoming clear, and since then the spread of mobile phones and use of the internet and email is obvious to all. The invention of Zuckerberg's Facebook in 2004, then Twitter in 2006, was not made in anticipation of revolutions, but in the hands of millions in North Africa in 2011 they found that destiny.

Anticipating a later chapter, concerning the taking of responsibility for defending, protecting and even developing the elementary natural and cultural conditions for a future truly human society (see my *Not_Without a Storm*), all attempts to combat the destruction of humanity consequent upon 'overdevelopment' contribute to the struggle for the future. The transition to socialism cannot happen without the creation (self-creation) in struggle of new men and women. This is the meaning of the young Marx's understanding of the necessity of a mass communist consciousness, a concept with which would-be Marxists have always had difficulty.

"Both for the production on a mass scale of this communist consciousness, and for the success of the cause itself, the alteration of men on a mass scale is necessary, an alteration which can only take place in a practical movement, a revolution; the revolution is necessary, therefore, not only because the ruling class cannot be overthrown in any other way, but also because the class overthrowing it can only in a revolution succeed in ridding itself of all the muck of ages and become fitted to found society anew."[10]

(b) 'Socialisation of production' and the precondition of communism

In order to understand the historical basis of what I have called 'overdevelopment', it is necessary to begin from what Marx meant by the 'socialisation of production' in capitalist society itself as the precondition of communism.

Communism, as conceived by Marx, far from having failed or been defeated, has never existed. Marx's ideas about communism, about capitalism and the alternative to it, are urgently relevant, indeed essential, if we are to understand and act against the dangers posed by 'globalised' capital to nature and to our future.

In trying to demonstrate the truth of these assertions I intend to rely to a great extent on Marx's own words. Marx had in a general way anticipated 'globalisation'. Thus, in the *Communist Manifesto*:

> Constant revolutionising of production, uninterrupted disturbances of all social conditions, everlasting uncertainty and agitation distinguishes the bourgeois epoch from all earlier ones. All fixed, fast-frozen and venerable prejudices and opinions, are swept away, all new-formed ones become antiquated before they can ossify. All that is solid melts into air, all that is holy is profaned, and man is at last compelled to

---

[10] Marx and Engels, *Collected Works*, Vol. 5, Lawrence & Wishart 1976, pp. 52-3

face with sober senses his real conditions of life, and his relations with his kind ....

The need of a constantly expanding market for its products chases the bourgeoisie over the entire surface of the globe. It must nestle everywhere, settle everywhere, establish connections everywhere.

The bourgeoisie has through its exploitation of the world market given a cosmopolitan character to production and consumption in every country .... All old-established national industries have been destroyed or are daily being destroyed. They are dislodged by new industries, whose introduction becomes a life and death question for all civilised nations... We find new wants, requiring for their satisfaction the products of distant lands ... In place of the old local and national seclusion and self-sufficiency, we have intercourse in every direction, universal interdependence of nations. (In Marx and Engels *Collected Works*, Vol. 6, p. 186)

And in 1858 Marx wrote to Engels a letter every word of which, from the standpoint of today, merits close study:

There is no denying that bourgeois society has for the second time experienced its sixteenth century which, I hope, will sound its death knell just as the first ushered it into the world. The proper task of bourgeois society is the creation of the world market, at least in outline, and of the production based on that market. Since the world is round, the colonisation of California and Australia and the opening up of China and Japan would seem to have completed this process. For us, the difficult question is this: on the Continent revolution is imminent and will, moreover, instantly assume a socialist character. Will it not necessarily be crushed in this little corner of the earth, since the movement of bourgeois society is still in the ascendant over a far greater area?

Marx did not start from an idealised picture of some future society. Before him, 'utopian socialists' like Robert Owen, Fourier and Saint-Simon had envisaged and written inspiringly about such a possibility, and had also made biting criticism of the existing capitalist order. But as Walter Benjamin was to put it, the followers of Saint-Simon, for example, 'anticipated the development of the global economy, but not the class struggle'. Marx, on the other hand, found in capitalist society itself the potential and necessity of a force, the working class, that would be driven to make a social revolution, taking the road to communism. Communism will be a revival, at an infinitely higher level of human achievement, of the solidarity, equality and reciprocity found in many early societies. Working-class revolution will be unlike all previous ones, because it will not be merely a political revolution to establish the rule of a new exploiting class. The working class does not have some new mode of exploitation that it seeks to impose. Its revolution will be a social revolution to put an end to class society and exploitation of man by man. The methods, consciousness and forms of organisation of those who fight for that revolution must be consistent with and contribute to the future communist society of freely associated individuals, creative on the basis of the productive and cultural powers developed through the centuries of civilisation.

In earlier revolutions, it was a question of one exploiting class establishing its own mode of exploitation as the central controlling force of the social metabolism, determining its form and relationship with nature. This ruling class found the political and ideological means to ensure its monopoly of the means of production. Only for the members of this class was there the chance of participation in the heritage of human culture. The mass, the direct producers, were exploited and deprived. The socialist revolution, on the other hand, places all humanity in a relation with nature and with the need to produce that is no longer mediated by class division. It opens up the prospect of relations between individuals which are not so mediated. It begins the abolition of privileged access to culture, opening it up to all.

For these reasons Marx called the social revolution 'the human revolution'. This revolution, said Marx, comes about – as did earlier ones – when the old production relations become a barrier to the development of the productive forces which have been developed within them. In the case of the revolution against capital, Marx saw, the productive forces and the 'universal intercourse' foreshadowed by the world market will have provided the basis for human liberation. Not only is the revolution the work of the exploited majority rather than of a new exploiting minority class; private property in the means of production will also be abolished. The creation and reproduction of the resulting social order will be the work of all, the association of free and equal individuals. It is not mediated by the necessities of a mode of exploitation of human being by human being, as it is in capitalism.

But any definition of communism remains abstract if we do not include why it is possible and how it is to be attained: 'If we did not find concealed in society as it is, the material conditions of production and the corresponding relations of exchange prerequisite for a classless society, then all attempts to explode it would be quixotic.' (*Grundrisse*, p. 159)

Central to the conditions which Marx knew were necessary within capitalist development for a communist future is, let us repeat, the existence of a social force generated by capitalism itself that will act to put an end to the rule of capital. Its contradictions notwithstanding, the capital system will not give way to a new social order automatically. There must develop in capitalist society a class of people whose experiences of exploitation and struggles against it drive them to recognise that they must and can make a revolution if their life is to be a human one. The 'structural antagonist' of capital, the force upon which it depends for its self-reproduction and expansion, is the working class whose labour-power it buys and exploits. Marx's work showed that the social order ruled by capital depends for its very existence and daily reproduction on the exploitation of the labour time of the dispossessed majority, the working class.

Today we must return to a consideration that could not be there for Marx in the nineteenth century. It is only in our own day that the destructive consequences of the capitalist mode of production and exchange have come to predominate over capitalism's role of preparing the productive conditions for a future socialist order. It would be a mistake to perpetuate the idea that science and technology as it exists and is organised in capitalism can simply be taken over as the basis for socialist production, because their development is grossly distorted by their monopolisation by capital and its imperative need to continually find ways of creating exchange-values (even when this means deliberately producing waste, or goods which are quickly destroyed or prematurely used up or rendered obsolete), as against the satisfaction of real needs. We have reached the point where the very future of humanity and of the environment is threatened by capital's uncontrolled exploitation of nature and of human beings in this pursuit of capital accumulation. And one consequence of this threat is that many, many people – scientists, writers, educators, artists and others, not by definition members of the working class - come to the side of the working class in the fight for a future, that communist future of freely associated individuals.

(c) The 'social brain'

Here the key is what Marx called the socialisation of production. Capital is the ruling power in today's societies. It is formed and accumulated by 'the theft of alien labour time'. That is to say, once the worker has added to a product's value enough to cover his own living wage, then the value added by his work to the product in the remaining time of his labour (surplus value) is acquired by his employer. It is value that the employer must then 'realise' in the sale of the commodity, and which thus results in accumulation of capital.

Marx showed that this mode of exploitation of labour, the very life-blood of capitalism, must more and more come into contradiction with 'the socialisation of production'. By the latter he meant the ever-increasing dependence of production on science, technology, machines. In this dependence (far more advanced today than in Marx's time) production is more and more governed and carried through not simply by the individual wage-labourer but by the products (machinery, etc) of 'the social intellect' or 'social brain', to use Marx's own words. That is to say: in technology is incorporated the accumulated knowledge, experience, science and technique of society.

But to the degree that large industry develops, the creation of real wealth comes to depend less on labour time and on the amount of labour employed than on the power of the agencies set in motion during labour time, whose 'powerful effectiveness' is itself out of all proportion to the direct labour time spent on their production, but depends rather on the general state of science and on the progress of technology, or the application of this science to production. (*Grundrisse* pp. 704-5)

It is obvious that no capitalist can compete and survive without investing in the developments achieved by this 'social brain'.

As for the wage labourer:

Labour no longer appears so much to be included within the production process; rather, the human being comes to relate more as watchman and regulator to the production process itself. The worker... steps to the side of the production process instead of being its chief actor. (Ibid.)

Far from bewailing this reduction of the worker to a mere onlooker, however, Marx finds here the key to the overcoming of capital's rule by the working class:

In this transformation, it is neither the direct human labour he himself performs, nor the time during which he works, but rather the appropriation of his own general productive power, his understanding of nature and his mastery over it by virtue of his presence as a social body – it is, in a word, the development of the social individual which appears as the great foundation-stone of production and of wealth.

And what truly is 'wealth'? In the present system of capital's rule, labour time and the 'theft' of it by capital as surplus value and for the accumulation of capital is the measure of wealth, and exchange-value is the measure of actual use-value. That is to say, use-values (wealth) are produced solely for their exchange-value (and can be obtained and used only if one has the money). Now, however, with the extraordinary development of machinery and information technology, 'labour in the direct form' plays a tiny and ever-diminishing part in the production of use-values, and is no longer in reality the real wellspring of wealth. It is now the 'development of the social individual', each one operating with and through the powers of the 'social brain' (Marx), that 'appears as the great foundation-stone of production and of wealth'. Communism will turn this socialisation of production 'the right way up', directing it to the overcoming of alienation.

Producing things as commodities, exchange-values, and confining the quantity and quality of that production within the limits of the requirements of maintaining and furthering the value-relation and profit, is more and more in irreconcilable conflict with the production of real wealth. Marx wrote in an early work, *The Poverty of Philosophy*: 'In a future society in which class antagonism will have ceased, in which there will no longer be any classes, use will no longer be determined by the minimum time of production; but the time of production devoted to an article will be determined by the degree of its utility.'[11]

Given that the ever-increasing socialisation of production is in conflict with 'theft of alien labour time' as the basis of the mode of production and self-reproduction of social life, surely there must be enormous implications of the hitherto unimaginable gain in time from information technology (IT). Do not these implications speak volumes for Marx's idea of communism as an association of creative free individuals? Marx concludes:

> ... the development of the productive forces brought about by the historical development of capital itself, when it reaches a certain point, suspends [i.e. negates and overcomes, CS] the self-realisation of capital, instead of positing it. Beyond a certain point, the development of the powers of production becomes a barrier for capital; hence the capital relation [becomes] a barrier for the development of the productive powers of labour. When it has reached this point, capital, i.e. wage labour, enters into the same relation towards the development of social wealth and of the forces of production as the guild system, serfdom, slavery, and is necessarily stripped off as a fetter. The last form of servitude assumed by

---

[11] In Marx and Engels, *Collected Works*, Vol 6, Lawrence & Wishart, 1976

human activity, that of wage labour on one side, capital on the other, is thereby cast off like a skin, and this casting off itself is the result of the mode of production corresponding to capital. (*Grundrisse*, p. 749.)

In several passages in the *Grundrisse* Marx returns to the fundamental question of socialisation of production. Here I give only one extract. A clear and detailed exposition can be found in Roman Rosdolsky's *The Making of Marx's 'Capital'*.

The development of fixed capital indicates to what degree general social knowledge has become a direct force of production, and to what degree, hence, the conditions of the process of social life itself have come under the control of the general intellect and been transformed in accordance with it.

(d) The social brain 'confined'

As society is now, this 'general social knowledge' as a force of production is appropriated piecemeal by capital and confronts the worker as fixed capital, alien to him, opposed to him, put in motion only to amass surplus value and not to serve humanity. This piling up of the 'monstrous' (Marx) alien power of the objective conditions of labour (conditions which are themselves the past product of labour itself) is essential to capital's modus operandi and has become global. This is the real meaning of 'globalisation', a globalisation within which capital '... wants to confine them (the "giant social forces") within the limits required to maintain the already created value as value. Forces of production and social relations – two different sides of the development of the social individual – appear to capital as mere means, and are merely means for it to produce on its limited foundation'.

István Mészáros sums up the formidable implications of this 'confining' of the giant social forces:

> ... the staggering productivity of capital enables it to swallow up the total material and human resources of our planet [the real root of the ecological crisis, CS] and vomit them out

again in the form of chronically under-utilised machinery and 'mass consumer goods', and much worse: immense accumulations of weaponry bent on destroying civilisation potentially a hundredfold. (*Beyond Capital*, p. 52)

And so we must go beyond Marx's insight that capitalism 'prepares the material conditions of emancipation': now 'capital's tremendous power of productivity' cannot be simply inherited by the 'new historical form'(i.e. socialism). Capital's now predominantly destructive mode of self-reproduction presents a 'Himalayan obstacle' (Mészáros) to the transition to socialism. Not only does it threaten the natural world and the material and cultural conquests of past generations; it produces pathological social results, with ever-intensifying problems of the composition and consciousness of the working class, as we have seen. We return to this aspect in later chapters.

For us it is the antagonism (dead versus living labour) that is the real source of the potential overcoming of capital – now patently a global task.

... the value objectified in machinery appears as a presupposition against which the value-creating power of the individual labour capacity (labour power) is an infinitesimal, vanishing magnitude. (*Grundrisse*, p. 695)

(This is the way to see the total production process today, in which computers etc. (machines) in London, Detroit or anywhere else in the world control the value-creating labour of countless billions as an 'infinitesimal, vanishing magnitude'.)

As for 'technological revolution' and all that, the real context is the contradiction between socialisation of production and private appropriation.

The action of a man, as the unique and 'entire connected act of production' (*Capital*, Vol. 2) is already more than the agent of this action.... The action already takes place in a higher sphere, which has the future for itself, the sphere of technics, while the agent of this action, as isolated individual, remains in the sphere of economics, and his product is likewise bound to this sphere.... Across the European continent, technology as a whole forms a single simultaneous action, insofar as it takes effect as technology; the physiognomy of the earth is from the outset transformed within the sphere of technics, and the gulf between city and country is ultimately spanned. But if the deadly force of economics should gain the upper hand, then the repetition of homologous magnitudes through absolutely interchangeable existences, the production of commodities through the agency of the worker, prevails over the singularity of the technological action. (Hugo Fischer, *Marx und sein Verhaltnis zu Staat und Wirtschaft*, quoted in Walter Benjamin, *The Arcades Project*, pp. 654-5)

To summarise, on the socialisation of production:

Production, the activity upon which all social life rests, is in our time totally dependent on the needs of capital, its need to extract surplus value from living labour and thus to accumulate more capital.

For this to be the case, there must exist an available supply of wage-labour, the working class, which, owning no means of production, must sell its labour-power. Thus the antagonism between capital and labour, between the capitalist class and the working class, is fundamental, structural.

Capital's own imperative demands have brought about a hitherto unimaginable socialisation of production, that is to say, an advance in science and technology meaning that production now depends not on the individual labourer's efforts but on the application of that science and technology, 'the social brain'.

But because capital and its accumulation need to rest on the theft of labour-time from workers, that need comes into contradiction with this infinite possibility of controlling the application of the social brain to production and the satisfaction of human needs, to the prospect of freedom. The need for wage-labour and of the structural division between a propertyless class and an employing class no longer exists historically. The existing class system becomes more and more a restriction on mankind's progress with the social brain, a destructive distortion of every use and product of its work. Simply, if humanity is to avoid destruction, the social brain and its work must be self-controlled, that is, controlled by society.

As we have seen (*Grundrisse*), '... if we did not find concealed in society as it is, the material conditions of production and the corresponding relations of exchange prerequisite for a classless society, then all attempts to explode it would be quixotic.' These material conditions are developed by capital in an inescapably contradictory way, coming into opposition to capital itself, and also in an inhuman way.

What is this barrier? What is 'the fundamental contradiction'?

> The stages of production which precede capital appear, regarded from its standpoint, as so many fetters upon the productive forces. It itself, however, correctly understood, appears as the condition of the development of the forces of production as long as they require an external spur, which appears at the same time as their bridle. It is a discipline over them, which becomes superfluous and burdensome at a certain level of their development, just like the guilds etc.' (*Grundrisse*, p. 415)

Marx was at pains to show that the 'universal intercourse' which is an indispensable element in communism is prepared by capital's own mode of self-reproduction, but comes into conflict with it. Thus:

> ... the universalising tendency of capital, which distinguishes it from all previous stages of production. Although limited by its very nature, it strives towards the universal development of the forces of production, and thus becomes the presupposition of a new mode of production, which is founded not on the development of the forces of production for the purpose of reproducing or at most expanding a given condition, but where the free, unobstructed, progressive and universal development of the forces of production is itself the presupposition of society and hence of its reproduction;

where advance beyond the point of departure is the only presupposition. (*Grundrisse*, p. 540)

The alienating, inhuman way in which these conditions are prepared is central to Marx's conception:

> The barrier to capital is that this entire development proceeds in a contradictory way, and that the working-out of the productive forces, of general wealth etc., knowledge etc., appears in such a way that the working individual alienates himself; relates to the conditions brought out of him by his labour as those not of his own but of an alien wealth and of his own poverty. But this antithetical form is itself fleeting, and produces the real conditions of its own suspension. (*Grundrisse*, p. 541)

Life itself has given us (2008-9) a fitting conclusion in the 'credit crunch', in which the furious and reckless market in debts sold on as 'securities' (*sic*) has produced the onset of mass sackings and closures. This is what Marx meant in writing of the absurdity of 'fictitious capital':

> ... interest-bearing capital, in general, is the fountainhead of all manner of insane forms, so that debts, for instance, can appear to the banker as commodities .... The insanity of the capitalist mode of conception reaches its climax here ... (*Capital*, Vol. 3, Part V, Foreign Languages Publishing House, Moscow, 1959)

Yes, 'insanity'.

> With the development of interest-bearing capital and the credit system, all capital seems to double itself, and sometimes treble itself, by the various modes in which the same capital, or perhaps even the same claim on a debt, appears in different forms in different hands. The greater part of this 'money-capital' is purely fictitious. (*Capital*, Vol. 3.)

The immediate causes of the banking, financial and consequent industrial and commercial crisis of 2008-9 and onwards, namely speculation, some it fraudulent, and the greed of banking and finance bosses, are just that: merely the immediate causes. But these arise from, are made possible by, and are but the outward and contemporary – and now 'overdeveloped' - form of the fundamental 'insanity' of capitalism and its development to 'fictitious' capital, as analysed by Karl Marx ... a long time ago.

Chapter 5
About Time ... and Free Time

(a) 'All real economy is economy of time'

The classical political economists cited by Marx were right to conclude that 'all real economy is economy of time'. Now, today, labour-time in many most important instances, and time of communication, control and response, are unimaginably and ever-increasingly reduced in comparison with Marx's day. This adds a massive new dimension to the question: what are the implications of Marx's conclusion that the socialisation of production and development of productive forces contradict and make historically redundant a system based on the theft of alienated labour-time?!

In his *Grundrisse*, Marx found it necessary to show in detail the significance of the means of transport and communication, and their costs, for the workings of capital. The advancing development of those means is of central importance:

> Capital by its nature drives beyond every spatial barrier. Thus the creation of the physical conditions of exchange – of the means of communication and transport – the annihilation of space by time – becomes an extraordinary necessity for it. (*Grundrisse*, p. 539)

To put the problem as sharply as possible: with the use of information technology this 'annihilation of space by time' reaches a qualitatively new level. It has accelerated to a previously unimaginable degree the globalisation of capital, and inevitably brings infinitely greater intensity to its workings and contradictions. The key to our twenty-first-century historical situation is the development of socialisation of production (the presence of the 'social brain' and its powers in every labour, every transaction), now at an entirely new, higher level.

The implications of these changes for the potential of what Marx called 'universal intercourse' and almost limitless 'free time' in the communist future surely need no emphasis – we will freely confront and participate in a world where science and technique are opening up, at an incredible speed, the past, the present and the future.

This very real potential for individuals' free and creative use of disposable time is completely stifled, suppressed, by the hierarchically imposed discipline of labour-time so necessary for capital's rule. And now that the productivity of labour is so vastly increased, and the truly necessary labour-time for production of use-values so vastly reduced, it becomes ever more inhuman and wasteful to subject men and women to a time-discipline in a productive process over whose purpose and execution they have no control whatsoever. Furthermore, there is no way in which the individual labourer can consciously and positively contribute his work and his motivation to the common interest. As Mészáros has insisted, this waste is at least as important as the more immediately recognised waste of energy and other resources in the prevailing socio-economic system.

Thus, the more the productivity of labour increases, the more capitalist society is faced with the contradiction between capital's fundamental need for surplus labour on the one hand and the potential of free time (great reduction of the working day) on the other. Why? Because capital must be put to work in order to appropriate the product of as much working time as possible, so that the time 'freed' by increased productivity of labour must be working time. Instead of the producers winning more free, disposable time for themselves from this greater productivity, they are in fact compelled to intensify their alienation. What clearer indication could there be of the contradiction between advanced productive forces and an outdated system of social relations which is based on the theft of the value created by labour-time?

This real 'anticipation' of the abundance of disposable time actually becomes more dangerous, dehumanising, so long as the rule of capital remains. First, and most obvious, is the fact that billions of working days as well as massive material resources are devoted to the production of waste, of goods and 'services' whose useful life is (preferably, from the point of view of capital) short, their characteristics quickly 'out of date'. As for the comically misnamed 'leisure industry' and the relatively higher disposable incomes in the advanced countries, one sees a distorted premonition of the 'disposable time necessary and possible in communism', but it is time and 'leisure' and apparent freedom without the cultured and associated individuals who should 'dispose' of it (not to mention unemployment, 'de-skilling', 'precarisation', stress, degrading occupations, etc., and of course the super-exploitation of the peoples of the 'third world').

The 'disposable time' potentially released by the vast increase in productivity of labour is devoted in large part to production of waste and artificial wants. It takes the inhumanly distorted form of unemployment and deprivation and today's 'leisure', with the time available for it and the products 'supplied' for it.

István Mészáros ends his pamphlet 'Unemployment and Casualisation: a Great Challenge to the Left' (no date) as follows:

> For due to the insurmountable constraints and contradictions of the capital system, any attempt at introducing disposable time as the regulator of social and economic interchanges – which would have to mean putting at the disposal of the individuals great amounts of free time, liberated through the reduction of working-time well beyond the limits of even a 20-hour working week – would act as social dynamite, blowing the established reproductive order sky high. For capital is totally incompatible with free time autonomously and meaningfully utilised by the freely associated individuals.

But the time released by the vastly increased productivity of labour remains imprisoned in the system ruled by capital. It must take the form of unemployment and deprivation, of casualisation, of the devotion of billions of working days to the production of deadly dangerous, shoddy and decadent goods and 'services' by people in unfulfilling, unskilled, super-exploitative and degrading jobs. That means 'social dynamite' in another sense, in that free time of this sort is 'incompatible' with any kind of social stability and accepted values and norms. That is the source of the daily media diet of crime, 'anti-social behaviour' and the furious outbursts of protest by ghetto-imprisoned young people, as in France. And we must add the cost in mental illness and wasted lives.

(b) Free time

Contrast the importance of time in communist society.

> On the basis of communal production, the determination of time remains, of course, essential. The less time the society requires to produce wheat, cattle etc, the more time it wins for other production, material or mental. (*Grundrisse*, pp. 172-3)

By contrast, in capitalism,

> Surplus time is the excess of the working day above that part of it which we call necessary labour time; it exists secondly as the multiplication of simultaneous working days, i.e. of the labouring population. (It can also be created ... by means of forcible prolongation of the working day beyond its natural limits; by the addition of women and children to the labouring population. (*Grundrisse*, pp. 704-5)

(Today we should add: and by incorporation of billions of new workers in the 'third world'.)

> Thus the first relation, that of the surplus time and the necessary time in the day, can be and is modified by the development of the productive forces, so that necessary labour is restricted to a constantly smaller fractional part. (*Grundrisse*, pp. 704-5)

This is the role of machinery, which increases the relation of surplus labour to necessary labour.

> Capital here – quite unintentionally – reduces human labour, expenditure of energy, to a minimum. This will redound to

the benefit of emancipated labour, and is the condition of its emancipation. (*Grundrisse*, pp. 704-5)

This emancipation is thus based above all on the possibility of free time arising from advance in the productive forces:

> But free time, disposable time, is wealth itself, partly for the enjoyment of the product, partly for free activity which – unlike labour – is not dominated by the pressure of an extraneous purpose which must be fulfilled, and the fulfilment of which is regarded as a natural necessity or a social duty, according to one's inclination.
>
> It is self-evident that if labour-time is reduced to a normal length and, furthermore, labour is no longer performed for someone else, but for myself, and, at the same time, the social contradictions between master and men, etc., being abolished, it acquires a quite different, free character, It becomes real social labour, and finally the basis of disposable time – the labour of a man who has also disposable time, must be of a much higher quality than that of the beast of burden. (Marx, *Theories of Surplus Value*, Foreign Languages Publishing House, Moscow, Part 3, p. 257)
>
> Free time – which is both idle time and time for higher activity – has naturally transformed its possessor into a different subject, and he then enters into the direct production process as this different subject. This process is then both discipline, as regards the human being in the process of becoming; and, at the same time practice (*Ausubung*), experimental science, materially creative and objectifying science, as regards the human being who has become, in whose head exists the accumulated knowledge of society.

Mészáros explains how capital negates the potential of higher productivity and free time:

> For capital is quite incapable of human considerations. It knows only one way of managing work-time: by maximally

exploiting the 'necessary labour time' of the workforce in employment, totally ignoring the available 'disposable time' in society at large, because it cannot squeeze profit out of it ... for capital's productive system de facto creates 'superfluous time' in society as a whole, on an ever-increasing scale. Yet it cannot conceivably acknowledge the *de jure* existence (i.e. the legitimacy) of such socially produced surplus-time as the potentially most creative disposable time we all have, which could be used in our society for the satisfaction of so much of the now cruelly denied human needs, from education and heath service requirements to the elimination of famine and malnutrition all over the world etc. (Mészáros, *The Challenge and Burden of Historical Time*, Monthly Review Press, 2008, p. 177)

(c) 'The annihilation of space by time'

Production, communication and control by information technology is surely such a 'development of the productive forces'. Once again, the development is contradictory, a development impelled by motives completely opposed to its potential for human freedom. For example:

... IBM's leadership in computer manufacture hung on the pathbreaking computers it built for the new computerised air defence system, SAGE; the semiconductor industry was brought into being by defence orders, which accounted for 38 per cent of all production between 1955 and 1965. (Will Hutton, *The World We're In*, Little, Brown, 2002, p. 153)

Here we reach the crux of our argument that socialisation of production and 'overdevelopment' are the key concepts for understanding our historical situation and the overcoming of its contradictions. The work for this small book began with the posing of what looked like a very difficult question, namely: given that computers and the 'information revolution' have reduced to an infinitesimal amount of time operations of communication, production and control, what in our day is the significance of the labour theory of value and of Marx's conclusion that the development of the productive forces, machines, has rendered redundant a system (the capital system) whose metabolism rests on 'the theft of alien labour time'? This he called the 'fundamental contradiction'.

Computers are machines, part of the productive forces. Their unimaginably greater speed of working than any earlier machines surely gives an entirely new dimension to that fundamental contradiction. At the touch of a keyboard, instantaneous results can be achieved anywhere in the world. In China, a country with many millions still living in primitive and brutal conditions, a 'supercomputer' has been produced which is capable of 563,000,000 calculations per second. Top of the world list is the American 'Jaguar', capable of 1,300,000,000 calculations per second.

Such is the magnitude of the changes being wrought by information technology. The scale of this factor in what I have called 'overdevelopment', its enormous intensification of capitalism's 'fundamental contradiction', raises to an excruciating level the necessity of surpassing the system based on 'the theft of alien labour time'. Because at this point we cannot overcome the capital system, then the contradictions of 'overdevelopment' must now take ever more destructive and perverse forms, of which the financial and economic collapse of 2008-9 was but a small manifestation. I cannot do better here than point to Don De Lillo's masterful tale (*Cosmopolis*, Picador, 2003) of a high-flying businessman destroyed by these distorted developments. His hero is here listening to his 'theoretical' adviser, who says:

> You know how shameless I am in the presence of anything that calls itself an idea. The idea is time. Living in the future. Look at those numbers running. Money makes time. It used to be the other way around. Clock time accelerated the rise of capitalism. People stopped thinking about eternity. They began to concentrate on hours, measurable hours, man-hours, using labour more efficiently.

The conversation continues:

> He said, 'There's something I want to show you.'
> 'Wait. I'm thinking'

He waited. Her smile was slightly twisted.
'It's cyber-capital that creates the future. What is the measurement called a nanosecond?" 'Ten to the minus ninth power.' 'This is what?'
'One billionth of a second,' he said.
'I understand none of this. But it tells me how rigorous we need to be in order to take adequate measure of the world around us.'
'There are zeptoseconds.' 'Good. I'm glad.'
'Yeptoseconds. One septillionth of a second.'
'Because time is a corporate asset now. It belongs to the free market system. The present is harder to find. It is being sucked out of the world to make way for the future of uncontrolled markets and huge investment potential. The future becomes insistent.'

And De Lillo's wonderful punch-line:

'This is why something will happen soon, maybe today,' she said, looking slyly into her hands. 'To correct the acceleration of time. Bring nature back to normal, more or less.'

Yes, the 'annihilation of space by time', as Marx called it, has finally resulted in a frantic, destructive self-reproduction of capital in which our present is 'sucked out of the world', sacrificed to 'future huge investment potential'. 'Something must happen soon … to bring nature back to normal, more or less.'

Chapter 6

Human Labour and its Future

'We presuppose labour in a form that stamps it as exclusively human. A spider conducts operations that resemble those of a weaver, and a bee puts to shame many an architect in the construction of her cells. But what distinguishes the worst architect from the best of bees is this, that the architect raises his structure in imagination before he erects it in reality. At the end of every labour-process, we get a result that already existed in the imagination of the labourer at its commencement.' (Marx, in *Capital*, Vol.1, Chapter 7)

(a) Living labour and dead labour

At this point we need to confront the most original and at the same time most difficult part of Marx's analysis in his Capital: the distinction between 'concrete' and 'abstract' labour.
The labour Marx writes about when he compares human labour to that of the spider is the basic distinguishing character of humans: our 'productive labour, this natural condition of human existence' (Engels).
But can we understand the labour of men and women in today's society ruled by capital as the basis of their social existence, their social relations, their relations to each other and to society? And

is it true now that 'at the end of every labour-process there is a result that already existed in the imagination of the labourer at its commencement'? For one thing, it is obvious that today's individual worker is only an operative in a work-process conceived, planned, set in motion, coordinated and completed at a level beyond individual knowledge, control or 'imagination'. But that is so because of advances in science and technique (advances which of course have been appropriated by capital and imposed on every individual worker). However, there is now another and fundamental difference from the simple labour-process.

In our society, the labourer's work in producing useful things ('productive labour, this natural condition of human existence') is not the basis of his social relations, his relation to his fellow-humans. On the contrary – and this is fundamental – his labour-power is not a power directed at free, truly human activity. His labour-power is reduced to being a commodity, to be bought and sold like any other commodity. It has a use-value, and that use-value is labour, productive labour. The employer buys the commodity labour-power (its price is a wage) and from then on possesses its use-value, to be used to produce useful things, to be sure; but besides the 'concrete' (particular) use-value of the product, the employer appropriates the value added to it by the worker's labour. This value is greater than the value of the commodity (labour-power) which he bought. Marx calls this difference surplus-value.

There are many and varied types of concrete labour, but they all have one thing in common: they are labours which produce not only useful things, use-values, but (actually above all, from the standpoint of capital) exchange-value. Marx showed that, 'abstracting' from the differences in types of useful, 'concrete' labour, we arrive at the common substance of them all and of their products. The world of commodities is a world where all human products, the results of all labours, are equal to each other in the sense that they are values, values which can be exchanged and accumulated as products of human labour as such, what Marx called abstract labour (i.e., abstracting from the different 'concrete' types of labour).

The capital system's whole life-process or metabolism – its process of daily reproduction as a system – is driven by the imperative to accumulate more and more surplus-value, which becomes capital. This capital, invested in plant, raw materials, machinery (constant capital) and in labour-power (variable capital – variable in that it brings about an increase in value) returns to the worker as an alien power to which he must sell himself if he is to live. In his way his own product has created a social relation external and alien to him, returning to exploit him once again.

On the basis of these basic discoveries and concepts of Marx we can see clearly the contrast between the basic and essential labour-process characterising humanity, on the one hand, and production as it has now become, on the other, production of surplus-value as dictated by the demands of capital.

Marx devotes many pages of his *Capital* to the importance of machinery in capitalist production. For capital, machinery is a means for shortening that part of the working day in which the value of the worker's labour-power is replaced, so that for a greater part of the day he is producing surplus-value. With machine production, the worker more and more becomes 'a mere appendage' of the means of production. The machine as an instrument of production, fixed capital, is of course itself the product of past labour, now in the shape of 'dead labour', confronting and 'pumping dry' the living labour of the worker. 'The special skill of each insignificant factory operative vanishes as an infinitesimal quantity before the science, the gigantic physical forces, and the mass of labour that are embodied in the factory mechanism and, together with that mechanism, constitute the power of the "master".'

This reduction of the labourer to an adjunct of the capital (capital is 'dead labour') embodied in machinery can be seen as the physical and immediately felt completion of the alienation of the wage-labourer, whose labour is used, its product appropriated, purely for the purpose of incorporating value in the product as a commodity. The reality that the labour of individuals was expended on the commodities produced is of course not apparent in those commodities. They have a use-value of whatever kind, and a value in exchange, expressed in price. That exchange-value appears to be a material property or characteristic of the commodity; it is in fact the expression of the labour contained in it. Instead of the fundamental social relation, we see a thing.

If this alienation is to be overcome, it is necessary that the producers become conscious of it. The men and women who produce society's wealth do not start with their own implements and the raw materials available in nature (or made available by past labour), nor with their own conception of what is to be produced and how. On the contrary, they can set to work only when they make themselves available to an employer, because the means of production and the raw materials extracted from nature are in the hands of the class of employers. (These resources, it should never be forgotten, do not 'naturally' take the form of capital; they were forcibly expropriated from the individuals and communities who formerly possessed them.)

The owners of capital confront workers not just as that class of people who have the financial wherewithal to pay wages. They confront them also as the 'personifications' of all the social powers of labour, of the productive forces historically developed by social labour. It is impossible to over-emphasise the fact that these are the powers (means and forces of production) of society – yet they can be called into life only according to the needs (economic imperatives) of capital, as conceived and acted upon by the minority which has appropriated that capital.

The whole meaning of socialism/communism is the overcoming of this alienation of individuals' essential powers, so that the preconditions of the daily reproduction of social life and culture exist as men's and women's own (communal) property, for the use of which they will have to devise collectively shared methods and decisions about priorities. It will be the restoration of the genuinely human form of labour, but collectively as well as individually.

It goes without saying that between our present situation and the realisation of such a prospect stand great obstacles that must be overcome. Not only do the 'personifications of capital' constitute also the politically ruling class, with all the state's powers of coercion at their disposal. To this must be added the impact upon consciousness of the reality of capital's all-pervading dominance. All manner of ideological forms, control of the media, educational conditioning, etc., as well as direct propaganda, as well as the compulsion and necessity of every day's work, flow from and sustain the existing social order. There can be no fundamental social change without the development of a consciousness of the inhuman (the word is used in its literal sense) nature of capital's usurpation of humanity's powers. The inevitable industrial and political struggles and protest movements of all kinds will need continuity, interconnection and new forms of organisation, and the constant and radical critique of the ruling ideology is essential for this to come about. Marx compared the worker's recognition of capital's usurpation of labour's powers to the slave's self-recognition of his individual humanity, a self-recognition which was to make impossible the continued existence of slavery. (I once devised a university lecture course entitled 'Is capitalism eternal?')

Thus, in the social system dominated by capital, the distinctive and fundamental human relation of individuals to nature (through their conscious productive activity) and to each other is distorted, inverted. Certainly, when individuals engage in work and in their everyday relations, they do so with consciousness, intention and will. But they contribute to a result and totality of their actions which then confronts them as something external, something which no one willed, independent of their wills, alienated from them, as if with the force of inescapable, inevitable, 'natural' necessities of life to which there is no alternative but to conform.

As Marx puts it:

> Their own collisions with one another produce an alien social power standing above them, produce their mutual interaction as a process and power independent of them ...

And

> The social relation of individuals to one another as a power over the individuals which has become autonomous, whether conceived as a natural force, as chance or in whatever other form, is a necessary result of the fact that the point of departure is not the free social individual. (*Capital*, Vol 1, chapter 15)

(b) Labour and communism

The contrast with the nature of labour in communism could not be sharper. And we surely must not be talking here only of alienation of the worker in the production process. There is now a considerable body of work by critical sociologists on growing alienation in social life as a whole.

It has often been said that Marx did not speculate about the communist future. However, he did give many clear indications of its fundamental meaning. For him, the overcoming of the alienation inherent in the rule of capital will mean, in communist society, '... the control over, and the productive application of the forces of Nature by society, and the free development of the social productive powers.' (*Capital*, Vol 1, p. 787)

> Within the cooperative society based on common ownership of the means of production, the producers do not exchange their products; just as little does the labour employed on the products appear here as the value of these products, as a material quality possessed by them, since now, in contrast to capitalist society, individual labour exists no longer in an indirect fashion, but directly as a component part of the total labour. (*Critique of the Gotha Programme*)

The contrast between labour in this 'cooperative society' and labour in a society ruled by capital is further developed in Marx's *Grundrisse* (Preparatory Materials). The social relations, including exchange, between individuals will have a truly communal character. People will set to work, not according to what some owner of capital decides is a product likely to render a profit, but according to 'communal needs' and 'communal purposes'. In capitalism, the individual's work becomes meaningful for others only 'after the fact', when mediated by the market through its exchange-value. In communism, the work of the individual is at the start communal, social, planned in accordance with need and shared aspirations.

Engels explains very clearly the profound implications for human existence of this contrast:

> In every society in which production has developed spontaneously ... the situation is not that the producers control the means of production, but that the means of production control producers... In making itself master of all the means of production to use them in accordance with a social plan, society puts an end to the former subjection of men to their own means of production. It goes without saying that society cannot be free itself unless every individual is freed. The old mode of production must therefore be revolutionised from top to bottom, and in particular the former division of labour must disappear. Its place must be taken by an organisation of production in which, on the one hand, no individual can throw on to the shoulders of others his share in productive labour, this natural condition of human existence; and in which, on the other hand, productive labour, instead of being a means of subjugating men, will become a means of their emancipation, by offering each individual the opportunity to develop all his faculties, physical and mental, in all directions and to the full – in which, therefore, productive labour will become a pleasure instead of being a burden. Today this is no longer a fantasy, no longer a pious wish. (*Anti-Duhring*, quoted to great effect by Cyril Smith in his *Communist Society and Marxist Theory*, Index Books, 1988, pp. 78-9)

This will mean a transformation of the nature of the division of labour. Here there are two things of the greatest importance. First: the replacement of the present hierarchical, domineering, external force of compulsion and control by methods of decision-making and control by the labourers themselves. And second, intimately linked with the first, the overcoming of the division between mental and manual labour. In the capital system, the 'subject' of the productive process is capital, through its 'personifications'. In the future society, the subject will be the 'social brain', this time owned and directed by society, that is, by the actual producers and not by capital. Education will of course be central here, so that the producers can take part in the decision-making process rather than be simply part of the calculations made from above. Naturally the individual labourer cannot have in his head the scientific and technical knowledge to direct his labour. That knowledge exists at the level of society, and social means must be found to involve him, as against his being merely an appendage of the machine. The worker will be educated and cultured in such a way as to assure 'the greatest possible development of his aptitudes', so that he does not always have to be tied to the same tasks (Marx: 'Constant labour of one uniform kind disturbs the intensity and flow of a man's animal spirits, which find recreation and delight in mere change of activity').

In the society which overcomes and replaces the rule of capital, the 'producer' (the worker) does not get 'reestablishment' of private property but 'individual property based on the acquisitions of the capitalist era: i.e. on cooperation and the possession in common of the land and of the means of production.'

How do the conditions for such 'individual property based on the acquisitions of the capitalist era' come into being? Marx says that 'the expropriation' of the capitalists 'is accomplished by the action of the immanent laws of capitalistic production itself, by the centralisation of capital.... The expropriators are expropriated.' (*Capital, Vol 1,* p788, Allen & Unwin, 1946, chapter 13)

But it is not only the 'expropriation' of the owners of capital that capitalist production prepares. Despite its own dependence on the unfreedom of the majority of mankind, it prepares at the same time the indispensable conditions for human freedom. The compulsive drive of capital for profit and accumulation at all costs had the uniquely positive and progressive effect of advancing mankind's productive forces to the level where the satisfaction of the basic necessities of life needs take only a small proportion of total productive capacity. And yet, billions of men, women and children lack the elementary requirements of daily life, and the ruthless plunder of nature's resources threatens our and our children's future, for all to see. To understand the implications of all this, is it any longer necessary to grasp the theoretical intricacies of Marx's theory that at a certain level of its development, the capitalist order must come into contradiction with the productive forces it has called into being?

There exists now a massive surplus of available labour-power beyond the needs of satisfying the daily subsistence of the human race. What is necessary, in this context, is to revolutionise the deployment of these productive resources in answer to basic human needs, instead of according to potential profit and capital accumulation. Beyond this, there exist already in abundance the means of satisfying human needs of the most varied kind. So long as capital remains in control, it will seek out and manufacture any needs (wants) from which a profit can be realised, so that 'beyond-subsistence' needs are catered for in a commercialised and corrupting market. Furthermore, the time released by the great reduction in time needed for meeting subsistence needs today takes the form of unemployment, casualisation and a media-corrupting 'leisure' (we hear even of a 'leisure industry'!). Once the capital relation is surpassed, and the social body asserts its own control over the productive forces, then we will realise (make real) the potential of free, disposable time made possible by those forces and by the means of universal communication which have been delivered by science and technique in answer to capital's drive for accumulation. Science and technology, the 'social brain', will be freed of the economic and political/military demands of capital, and become the resource for the expansion of free choice, discovery and the creation and satisfaction of new needs.

Thus the contradictions of capitalism, for so long only a concept in the realm of theory and the vaguely understood culprit of recurrent crises, emerge more and more into the light of day as the basic content of our historical situation and destiny. The same social system in which the great majority has been exploited and oppressed has reached the stage – its historical/structural crisis – where its continued existence threatens the near future of everyone. And yet it has created, hidden behind that crisis, the material means for true freedom: freedom to utilise free time, freedom for creative activity beyond the satisfaction of material need, freedom to use the new means of communication to become 'universal individuals', freedom to restore labour to its true and uniquely human character. Individuality will then develop creatively, not in opposition to others but in a harmony where every individual can partake of the richness of all cultures and have the chance to make creative contributions to our cultural heritage.

Chapter 7

Individuals

(a) The individual and 'real wealth'

The commonly held idea that communism negates individual freedom is in fact the opposite of the truth. In point of fact, such negation is a fundamental characteristic of the rule of capital.

Because the individual's product, in capitalist society, becomes available for use, and available to his fellow-humans, it is alienated from him and must take the form of exchange-value, a commodity. The individual exists 'only as a producer of exchange-value' (Marx). None of this is decided by the individual, but is determined entirely historically, by the structure of the society into which s/he is born. Individuality can be sought only in a fight against, or for some escape from, this compulsion – an escape possible only on the basis of riches, or at the cost of social isolation.[12]

Marx in his early writings already insisted on this. In his 'Comments on James Mill', early in 1844, he wrote:

---

[12] '... the presupposition of exchange value, as the objective basis of the whole of the system of production, already in itself implies compulsion over the individual, since his immediate product is not a product for him, but only *becomes* such in the social process, and since it *must* take on this general but nevertheless external form; and that the individual has an existence only as a producer of exchange value, hence that the whole negation of his natural existence is already implied; that he is therefore entirely determined by society; that this further presupposes a division of labour etc., in which the individual is already posited in relations other than that of mere *exchanger*, etc. That therefore this presupposition by no means arises either out of the individual's will or out of the immediate nature of the individual, but that it is, rather, *historical*, and posits the individual as already *determined* by society.' (Marx, *Grundrisse*, pp. 247-8)

> Let us suppose that we had carried out our production as human beings ... My work would be a free manifestation of life, and hence an enjoyment of life... The specific nature of my individuality ... would be affirmed in my labour, since the latter would be an affirmation of my individual life. (Marx and Engels *Collected Works* (MECW), Vol. 3, Lawrence & Wishart, 1975, pp. 227-8)

One year later in *The German Ideology* (1845), again:

> The transformation, through the division of labour, of personal power into material powers, cannot be dispelled by dismissing the general idea from one's mind, but can only be abolished by the individuals again subjecting these material powers to themselves and abolishing the division of labour. This is not possible without the community. Only within the community has each individual the means of cultivating his gifts in all directions; hence personal freedom becomes possible only within the community. In the previous substitutes for community, in the state, etc., personal freedom has existed only for the individuals who developed under the conditions of the ruling class, and only insofar as they were individuals of this class. The illusory community in which individuals have up till now combined always took on an independent existence in relation to them, and since it was the combination of one class over against another, it was at the same time for the oppressed class not only a completely illusory community, but a new fetter as well. In the real community the individuals obtain their freedom in and through their association. (MECW, Vol. 5, pp. 77-8)

And

> ... the real intellectual wealth of the individual depends entirely on the wealth of his real connections. Only this will liberate the separate individuals from the various national and local barriers, bring them into practical connection with the production (including intellectual

production) of the whole world and make it possible for them to acquire the capacity to enjoy this all-sided production of the whole earth (the creations of man). All-round dependence, this primary natural form of the world-historical cooperation of individuals, will be transformed by the communist revolution into the control and conscious mastery of those powers, which, born of the action of men on one another, have till now overawed and ruled men as powers completely alien to them. (Ibid, p. 51)

As we noted above, Marx saw that the development of 'the social brain' as the basis of production must overcome the situation where intellectual and creative activity was made possible for the few by the labour of the many. On the new 'foundation-stone', we have

> The free development of individualities, and hence not the reduction of necessary labour time so as to posit surplus labour, but rather the general reduction of the necessary labour of society to a minimum, which then corresponds to the artistic, scientific etc. development of the individuals in the time set free, and with the means created, for all of them. (*Grundrisse*, p. 706)

Clearly it is a misapprehension to suppose that in his later work, Marx somehow left behind his ideas as a kind of abstract humanism. A reading of the *Grundrisse* dispels any such notion, as other passages like the following clearly show.

> Indifference towards specific labours corresponds to a form of society in which individuals can with ease transfer from one labour to another, and where the specific kind is a matter of chance for them, hence of indifference. Not only the category, labour, but labour in reality has here become the means of creating wealth in general, and has ceased to be organically linked with particular individuals in any specific form. Such a state of affairs is at its most developed in the most modern form of existence of bourgeois society – in the United States. (p. 101)

(How much more developed today!)

At the same time, in the 'advanced' countries, the sphere of consumption has a more and more contradictory character. Marx had already noted this contradictory character, and did not share the one-sided criticism of 'consumerism' made by many of today's Marxists. As David MacGregor writes in his *The Communist Ideal in Hegel and Marx* (University of Toronto Press, 1984, p. 210):

> Projecting the view of Hegel and classical Marxism, widening consumer choice in contemporary civil society, greater flexibility in purchases, and increased access to production and goods made possible by rising incomes and extension of consumer credit to the working class, are not portents of capitalism's decline, but rather necessary and predictable moments of bourgeois production itself. These developments may also anticipate a future 'free goods' society, where consumption will be disciplined and controlled by the cultured and civilised consciousness of the social individual.

Marx says that the capitalist

> searches for means to spur [the worker] on to consumption, to give his wares new charms, to impose them with new needs by constant chatter etc. It is precisely this side of the relation of capital and labour which is an essential civilising moment, and on which the historic justification, but also the contemporary power of capital rests. (*Grundrisse*, p. 287)

For Marx, while under capitalism the all-round, social interdependence of individuals took the form of a sphere external to and alienated from workers, nonetheless it was at the same time the basis of a 'personal independence' which could only be fully realised in communism. Then there will be 'free individuality, based on the universal development of individuals and their subordination of their communal, social productivity as their social wealth.' (*Grundrisse*, p. 158)

(b) The conditions for 'universally developed individuals'

For Marx, then, commodity production and exchange and money are essential to prepare the conditions of communism and 'universally developed individuals'.

> Universally developed individuals, whose social relations, as their own communal relations, are hence also subordinated to their own communal control, are no product of nature, but of history ... The degree and the universality of the development of wealth where this individuality becomes possible supposes production on the basis of exchange values as a prior condition, whose universality produces not only the alienation of the individual from himself and from others, but also the universality and the comprehensiveness of his relations and capacities. In earlier stages of development the single individual seems to be developed more fully, because he has not yet worked out his relationships in their fullness, or erected them as independent social powers and relations opposite himself. It is as ridiculous to yearn for a return to that original fullness as it is to believe that with this complete emptiness history has come to a standstill. (*Grundrisse*, p. 162)

Capitalism replaced personal dependence/domination with social power represented by a thing (money), which all possess. 'Rob the thing of this social power and you must give it to persons to exercise over persons'!! (Ibid, p. 158)

This is surely the clue to the economically backward and isolated Soviet Russia's inability to overcome 'the Great Russian bully' and autocratic/bureaucratic state!

> Strike out money, and one would thereby either be thrown back to a lower stage of production (corresponding to that of auxiliary barter), or one would proceed to a higher stage, in which exchange value would no longer be the principal aspect of the commodity, because social labour, whose representative it is, would no longer appear merely as socially mediated private labour. (Ibid, p. 214)

Marx went to great pains to express his conclusion that only through capitalism were the conditions for communism, freedom and true individuality (not individualism) being established. Capital cannot but drive to 'the exploration of the earth in all directions, to discover new things of use as well as new qualities of the old; such as new qualities of them as raw materials etc; the development, hence, of the natural sciences to their highest point.' From this flows

> ... likewise the discovery, creation and satisfaction of new needs arising from society itself; the cultivation of all the qualities of the social human being, production of the same in a form as rich as possible in needs, because rich in qualities and relations – production of this being as the most total and universal social product, for, in order to take gratification in a many-sided way, he must be capable of many pleasures, hence cultured to a high degree – is likewise a condition of production founded on capital... a constantly expanding and constantly enriched system of needs ... (Ibid, p. 542)

Capital's own imperatives create these necessary conditions for freedom, but they are conditions which develop in such a way as to negate the capital system itself:

> The universality towards which [capital] strives encounters barriers in its own nature, which will, at a certain stage of its development, allow it to be recognised as being itself the greatest barrier to this tendency, and hence will drive towards its own suspension [i.e., negation, overcoming: the German word is *aufhebung*]. (ibid, p. 410)

> The barrier to capital is that this entire development proceeds in a contradictory way, and that the working-out of the productive forces, of general wealth etc., knowledge etc., appears in such a way that the working individual alienates himself; relates to the conditions brought out of him by his labour as those not of his own but of an alien wealth and of his own poverty. But this antithetical form is itself fleeting, and produces the real conditions of its own suspension. (ibid, pp. 541-2)

Chapter 8

The 'human revolution' ... and the modern family?

Inevitably, since the crisis humanity faces is not a merely temporary one, capable of being solved within the capital system's own parameters, but a historical, structural crisis of the system as a system, it is manifested in a crisis of the 'cellular form' of capitalist society, the family.

Proceeding from Marx's idea that the social revolution to end capitalism and begin building a new society is 'the human revolution', Frederick Engels devoted his last work to the origin and nature of the family, private property and the state. His conclusions are directly relevant to an understanding of the present condition and the future of today's society and the place within it of the modern family.

The patriarchal family, including our own monogamous 'nuclear' family, has its origins conjointly with private property, class society and the state (Engels). Can it outlast these? Are they its very foundation? Has it (can it now have?) other foundations/*raisons d'être*?[13]

---

[13] 'We are now approaching a social revolution in which the economic foundations of monogamy as they have existed hitherto will disappear as surely as those of its complement, prostitution. Monogamy arose from the concentration of considerable wealth in the hands of a single individual – a man – and from the need to bequeath this wealth to the children of that man and of no other. For this purpose, the monogamy of the woman was required, not that of the man. So this monogamy of the woman did not in any way interfere with open or concealed polygamy on the part of the man. But by transforming by far the greater portion, at any rate, of permanent, inheritable wealth – the means of production – into social property, the coming social revolution will reduce to a minimum all this anxiety about bequeathing and

Capitalism is the last class society. Within capitalism the necessary conditions for the overcoming of class society, private property and the state mature. And the family?

'Universal intercourse' and highly developed productive forces have indeed reached the point where their contradiction with the metabolism of the capitalist mode of production (the theft of alien labour time) makes the self-reproduction of capital predominantly destructive.

No one any longer doubts that there is a real threat of the destruction of the planet's environment. The production of goods intended to be wasted (e.g. especially arms production) more and more predominates. Mankind's progress in achieving a more and more varied and efficient production of durable goods, as against the almost exclusive emphasis on immediately consumable products, is thus reversed by late capitalism. This is the articulation of capital's structural crisis.

(a) Crisis of the modern family

This structural crisis is not only economic, but political, ideological and moral, socially all-pervasive. One very important aspect of this crisis of culture is that (especially in the richest capitalist countries, but also in the rapidly emerging capitalist states like Russia and China) the purchasing power of individuals, the decline of old value-systems, and the increasingly dominant individualist ideology, 'free' individuals from old dependences, constraints and responsibilities, including those pertaining to sexual behaviour, marriage and the family. In varying forms and degrees, given 'globalisation', this is true of all societies, not only the 'overdeveloped' ones on which I concentrate here. And this variety is a rich field for study.

On the one hand, capital's own necessary development of productive forces and universal intercourse ('socialisation of production') is creating the preconditions for true individuality and freedom – the individuality and freedom of cultured and creative

---

inheriting. Having arisen from economic causes, will monogamy then disappear when these causes disappear?' (Engels, *Origin of the Family, Private Property and the State*. P. 81)

individuals in a society rid of exploitation. On the other hand, capital and its imperatives still rule our lives, so that these preconditions are at our disposal only in a truncated, distorted, primitive, individualistic, uncultivated and uncultured way (and in the final analysis, like capital's self-reproduction itself, a destructive way).

The opening up of a tawdry access to the consumer market (and what a market!) to masses of people, who must be persuaded to spend and spend again ('for the health of the economy', you understand), is not at all the opening of the door to that material well-being which in times past provided the possibility of a cultured and creative life for some scions of the bourgeoisie and the aristocracy, but the very opposite. It is a corruption, part of the alienation inevitable when human beings are dominated, as in the capital system, by their own product appropriated, 'realised' in money and then used to exploit them. The aspirations inspired and manipulated by the thousands of crude and disembodied images presented by advertising and 'reality TV' produce in the consumer not freedom but illusion and social isolation. Here we can see the increasing misuse of the internet, with massive consumer mechanisms, and mountains of 'spam', 'phishing', and millions of pornographic images. In 2006, there were 4.2 million pornography sites, with an estimated revenue of over 100 billion dollars (300 dollars per second), greater than the revenues of the top 10 technology companies combined.

The crisis of the modern family and of its attendant codes of fidelity, morality and responsibility, and the availability of money, give men (and to a much lesser extent, women) an illusory liberation. More and more, they can make decisions – risk separation, divorce, abandon their children – of their own 'free will'.

Thus: because of what capitalism can now offer (and this access to the market which it offers is something that capital *needs* to offer), men (and, again, to a lesser extent, women) are 'free' to make what interpersonal relationships they can. To reiterate: this is not because of liberating social change but because of the material forces of production and capacity for consumption generated by capitalism. The social/cultural relations (communism) necessary to realise and release these productive forces, these great gains for human progress, do not yet exist. Capital remains the ruler, and the society/'community'(*vide* Thatcher!) is no community at all; and the individuals in it are not free but imprisoned.

The monogamous family is not only the social institution for the perpetuation of private ownership of property, and in particular of capital (Engels). It is, for capitalism, the unit for reproduction of the most important commodity of all, labour-power, i.e., for the continued existence of a propertyless proletariat, of the essential class system. And as the principal mode of transmission of values and norms to effect control of the younger generation, it is surely collapsing, which is 'dangerous' (hence the solemn pronouncements of government ministers and church pontiffs).

The so-called generation gap is every day widened by the inability of the system to guarantee jobs for young people, ending the traditional transition from school to work, and at the same time looking to the youth as one of the mainstays of the consumer market. At the other end of the scale, enforced early retirement means that millions more people are forced into inactivity, the attack on their pensions adding insult to injury.

Thus the capitalist order needs the nuclear family as the cellular unit of society, but today capital in the overdeveloped countries has other 'needs' – to have millions of women available as cheap and easily 'casualised' labour, to destroy the innocence of youth through ruthless exploitation of the consumer market, to create enormous problems of 'affording' care for the elderly, who constitute an ever-growing proportion of the population, to ignore morality where it interferes with sales. These 'needs' systematically undermine the nuclear family.

This is why the family occupies a central position in the whole argument advanced in these notes. First, the family inevitably finds ·itself at the focus of all the problems of 'overdevelopment' and its pathological results, and yet it is the cellular unit where the subsistence of the bearers of labour-power and its reproduction must take place, thus it is structurally necessary to capital, despite the fact that capital at its latest stage must undermine it. And second, the family and its future are necessarily at the centre of that necessary historical change which we have characterised as the 'human revolution'.

It is not surprising, then, that the 'neo-liberal' offensive of the last quarter of the twentieth century included a reactionary re-assertion of 'family values'. Women had begun to rebel against their subordinate role in the nuclear family, where they were in effect reduced to the unpaid labour of maintaining and reproducing the supply of labour-power. Women were wanting the right to independence, to work, to pay, and to control over their own bodies. They wanted equality, liberation.

(b) From the first 'human revolution' to the second

We can say that so far as relations of dominance between the sexes is concerned, as in every other way, the 'dehumanisation' which has always been one side of life in class society (in particular of course for the exploited classes) reaches its very depths in capitalism, where use-value is subordinated to exchange-value, productive labour subordinated to the accumulation of value (and the self-expansion of capital), the worth of an individual reduced to his/her usefulness in rendering surplus value to an alien power, capital.

In the socialist society which follows capitalism, the monogamous family will no longer be required as the reproductive framework for the commodity labour-power or the inheritance of private property. Production will be the production of use-values by free individuals as participants in the working of the 'social brain'. How these individuals will be reared and formed will be an entirely new question, to be taken up by free men and women. As Lewis Henry Morgan concluded in 1877:

> When the fact is accepted that the family has passed through four successive forms, and is now in a fifth, the question at once arises whether this form can be permanent in the future. The only answer that can be given is that it must advance as society advances, and change as society changes, even as it

has done in the past. It is the creature of the social system, and will reflect its culture. As the monogamian family has improved greatly since the commencement of civilisation, and very sensibly in modern times, it is at least supposable that it is capable of still further improvement until the equality of the sexes is obtained. Should the monogamian family in the distant future fail to answer the requirements of society, assuming the continuous progress of civilisation, it is impossible to predict the nature of its successor. (*Ancient Society*, Bahrab Library, Calcutta, Part III, Chapter 5)

Morgan was just as enlightened on the question of the nature of the 'society of the distant future':

A mere property career is not the final destiny of mankind, if progress is to be the law of the future as it has been of the past. The time which has passed away since civilisation began is but a fragment of the past duration of man's existence: and but a fragment of the ages yet to come. The dissolution of society bids fair to become the termination of a career of which property is the end and aim; because such a career contains the elements of self-destruction. Democracy in government, brotherhood in society, equality in rights and privileges and universal education, foreshadow the next higher plane of society to which experience, intelligence and knowledge are steadily tending. It will be a revival, in a higher form, of the liberty, equality and fraternity of the ancient *gentes*.' (Ibid, Part IV, Chapter 1)

Against the dehumanisation wrought by the rule of capital, another 'human revolution' (Marx), like the first one that made us humans, is necessary. Every day it becomes more clear that the rule of capital, its inexorable drive for expanded self-reproduction through the exploitation of nature and of human beings, is predominantly destructive of precisely what is human, at the centre of which is our unique and creative relation to nature.

Every step in the natural and historical sciences which adds to our understanding of what is distinctively human should deepen our understanding of what the 'human revolution' will mean. Homo sapiens is physically unique, as is every other species, but our relation to nature, our mode of staying alive, is qualitatively different from that of any other species. It is not regulated by inherited, automatic, instinctive exchanges with the rest of nature. The necessary physical, biological, chemical exchanges with nature are achieved through social labour. The daily reproduction of life depends on this labour. It is social labour, i.e., the means and methods of doing it are not individual but require a system of relations between the individuals and a historically acquired culture (in particular a division of labour), a mode of production.

The transition to the human required certain physical, biological, genetic advances (erect posture, opposable finger and thumb, thin cranium, a more complex brain with greatly increased learning capacity, etc.). The human child needs maternal care for a much longer time than in other species, which has obvious implications for the kind of domestic life and family. Archaeological discoveries show us that the using and making of tools occurs in a social context. For the means of communication (language and ritual) essential for the social and cultural existence unique to our species to come into being, much larger brains, capable of a new kind of consciousness, were of course essential.

For the brains of the first human children to develop, a great change in the work of women was involved. Not only are human offspring incapable of independent activity and self-preservation for far longer than are the offspring of any other species; several years of childcare are necessary for learning to take shape. Women would still do a certain amount of food-gathering, but in the climatic conditions of the onset of the last Ice Age in which modern humanity emerged (the Upper Palaeolithic in Europe, some 100,000 years earlier in Africa), diet had to be supplemented by meat, and that meant that mothers and their children must have a settled social relationship with males, who were free from the responsibilities of childcare and hunted big game. These early humans learned to live in settled rather than nomadic conditions, in small communities based on common matrilineal descent (matrilineal clans or *gentes* (singular *gens*). Exogamy and a ban on incest were the rules. There had to be solidarity and controlled sharing by the members of these descent-groups (not individual bargains of individual women with individual males). This revolution, as well as the ability to use and develop advanced stone tools, was essential to the establishment of truly human society and culture, overcoming a simply animal interchange with nature. Now there had to be cultural continuity, achieved at that early stage by ritual. This cultural continuity, this solidarity, community and equality, were at the very root of 'becoming human'. They have to be revived in the higher forms made possible by millennia of our ancestors' achievements, in a new 'human revolution' to overcome the dehumanisation now inflicted on us by the rule of capital.

For tens of thousands of years these social systems based on kinship and territorial groupings survived, adapting subsistence production to varied environments and natural resources and with a wide variety of forms of social organisation. They gave way, with the development of agriculture in especially favourable conditions, to the possibility of production of a surplus, and thus to societies with private property, social classes and the exploitation of man by man. The archaeological record shows that it is only some 6,000 years ago that such societies were firmly established, in India and the Middle East.

With private property and the imperative of its being inherited came the return of the oppression of women. The fundamental humanity of the first 'human revolution' came under permanent attack, with exploitation of the direct producers and the subordination of women in the patriarchal family. Since then, 'the history of all societies has been the history of class struggle'.

In the last of these class-divided societies, capitalism, the social nature of production develops to the point where it comes into extreme contradiction with private property in the means of production and the exploitation of the direct producers. And here we arrive at that 'socialisation of production' so central to Marx's theory. Every act of labour calls into play the body of knowledge and practice of society, the 'social brain', even though the resources of this brain are appropriated and commanded piecemeal as fixed capital, when they patently require social control.

This collective control will restore a relation of humans to the rest of nature which nurtures nature, not exploits it, and which nurtures humans and their relations with each other, instead of exploiting them. And so, once more, the socialist revolution is not the replacement of one form of class rule by another, but the human revolution, just as was the first human revolution (at the origin of human society and culture). Just as then, the liberation of women is central to it.

Why is the crisis of the modern family fundamental to our central preoccupation, the socialisation of production, its 'overdevelopment' and the historical contradiction which must therefore be resolved? The 'human revolution' that made possible community and culture was eventually followed by the transition to the nuclear family dominated by the male, together with private property. This 'world historical defeat of the female sex' (Engels) can be called 'counter-revolutionary'. Capitalism is the last of the class societies which resulted. Today, among the pathological results of capitalism's overdevelopment are the commodification of sex and the illusory freedom of divorce and multiple relationships. The nuclear family, embedded in the dominance of men, is breaking up, and the broken-up men and women find themselves in a world where society is not community, and there remain only fragmentary communities (whereas the first human revolution embedded sexual relations in community).

Again, then, the conditions for the abolition of want and mutual cooperation have matured, indeed overdeveloped, and the contradiction between this socialisation of production and the capitalist mode of production endangers humanity. Just as a revolution – the first human revolution – was necessary in order for 'society to organise sex' and achieve the beginning of culture, so now another revolution is necessary to restore society's self-control. As in the original human revolution, it will require the organisation and collective consciousness of men and women to overcome the contradictions we have described and to build the new order.

(c) Has the family a future?

Our first question, 'has the family a future?' has not been answered. It is surely right to leave it as a question, limiting ourselves to outlining as best we can the dimensions and interconnnections of the question. This suggests certain pointers, for example:

- male supremacy will come to an end;
- for free men and women, individual sex love (the full flowering of which is obstructed, even made impossible for many, by the existing exploitative social relations) will surely have the chance to flourish and bring new gifts;
- individuals' freedom to decide, in truly human conditions, will bring results beyond our ken;
- much more will be learned about the needs of children.

In any case, it is certain that there will be great variety in how individuals choose to share their lives. Surely the best answer comes again from Engels and Morgan:

> Full freedom of marriage can therefore only be generally established when the abolition of capitalist production and of the property relations created by it has removed all the accompanying economic considerations which still exert such a powerful influence on the choice of a marriage partner. For then there is no other motive left except mutual inclination. (*Origin of the Family, Private Property and the State*, Lawrence & Wishart, 1940, p. 88)

To summarise:

Natural evolution resulted in the emergence of humans, a qualitatively new species in the sense that humans are equipped with the potential ability to relate to the rest of nature in an entirely new way. They did not relate to nature but began to transform one part of nature (tool-making) and use it to take their means of life from the rest of nature.

By a 'human revolution' I mean a revolution made by humans. In the first human revolution, humans devised social relations in accordance with their primitive means of production (tools). This social framework was in a certain sense a 'natural' one, based on kinship and descent. These kin-relations were organised socially. Such kinship and descent systems served human society for millennia, in all kinds of natural environments and with varying types of production, from food-gathering and hunting to pastoralism and subsistence agriculture. There were and are survivals of such systems of consanguinity and affinity in civilised societies but they do not organise any such society as a whole.

With settled populations based on agriculture and under exceptionally favourable conditions of fertility came the possibility of a surplus product and the appropriation of that surplus by a ruling class. Thus in the Near East and India there is clear evidence of a transition from village agriculture to class-divided urban society and state based on large-scale agriculture, between 8000 and 4000 BC. With surplus product came the possibility of trade and the accumulation of wealth through trade, and this was a vital element in the development of early civilisations and in some cases of the relations between them.

The next, second human revolution must be, once again, the creation by humans of a system of social relations which are appropriate for the fulfilment of the promise of the productive forces now developed. These productive forces are entrapped in a system of social metabolism dependent on the needs of capital, not of human beings. The contradiction between productive forces and production relations has reached the point where the self-reproduction of capital (the driving-force of the whole system) has become destructive, to the point of threatening the very basic relation between humanity and the rest of nature. The transition from this rule of capital to a society where free men and women control their own destiny – that will be our human revolution.

We should be in no doubt about the absolutely fundamental nature of this question. This was heavily emphasised by Marx in his early writings:

> In the approach to *woman* as the *spoil* and handmaid of communal lust is expressed the infinite degradation in which man exists for himself, for the secret of this approach has its *unambiguous*, decisive, *plain* and undisguised expression in the relation of *man* to *woman* and in the manner in which the *direct* and *natural* species-relationship is conceived .... From this relationship one can therefore judge man's whole level of development.[14]

(d) Note: Some opinions on the family and marriage

Mary Wollstonecraft: 'I do not wish women to have power over men; but over themselves.' (*A Vindication of the Rights of Women*, 1792)

Marx and Engels: '... Property, the first form of which lies in the family, where wife and children are the slaves of the husband.' (*The German Ideology*, 1846. In MECW, Vol.5, p. 46)

Frederick Engels: 'For the first time man, in a certain sense, is finally marked off from the animal kingdom, and emerges from mere animal conditions of existence into really human ones.' (*Anti-Duhring*, 1878. In MECW, Vol 25, p. 270)

Engels: 'The overthrow of mother-right was the world-historical defeat of the female sex. The man took command in the home also; the woman was degraded and reduced to servitude, she became the slave of his lust and a mere instrument for the production of children. This degraded position of the woman, especially conspicuous among the Greeks of the heroic and still more of the classical age, has gradually been palliated and glazed over, and sometimes clothed in a milder form; in no sense has it been abolished....

'Having arisen from economic causes, will monogamy then disappear when these causes disappear? One might answer, not without reason: far from disappearing, it will, on the contrary, be realised completely. For with the transformation of the means of production into social property there will disappear also wage labour, the proletariat, and therefore the necessity for a certain – statistically calculable – number of women to surrender themselves for money. Prostitution disappears; monogamy, instead of collapsing, at last becomes a reality – also for men.' (*Origin of the Family, Private Property and the State*, 1884, p. 81)

August Strindberg: 'Family .... The home of all social evil, a charitable institution for comfortable women, an anchorage for housefathers, and a hell for children.' (*The Son of a Servant*, 1886)

---

[14] *Economic and Philosophical Manuscripts of 1844*, in MECW, Vol 3, Lawrence & Wishart, 1975, pp. 295-6

Oscar Wilde: 'In married life three is company and two none.' (*The Importance of Being Earnest*, 1895)

Thornton Wilder: 'Marriage is a bribe to make a housekeeper think she is a householder.' (*The Merchant of Yonkers*, 1939)

Attributed to Mae West or Groucho Marx: 'Marriage is an institution, but who wants to live in an institution?'

Edmund Leach: 'Far from being the basis of the good society, the family, with its narrow privacy and tawdry secrets, is the source of all our discontents.' (Reith Lecture 1967, *The Listener*, November 1967)

Margaret Thatcher: 'There is no such thing as Society. There are individual men and women, and there are families.' *Woman's Own*, 31 October 1987)

Chapter 9
Revolutionary agency: the theoretical framework

In the following chapters (10 and 11) I return to the question raised at the conclusion of Chapter 1: how can we approach the crucial question of the agency for the social revolution, and why should we begin from the conviction that working class must be its agent? But it is first necessary, in the present chapter, to outline the theoretical basis for an answer. In Chapter 6, the central role of labour in human life, and the contrast between labour under the rule of capital and in a future socialist/communist society was outlined, and it is this thread that must now be taken up.

Why did Marx and Engels insist that the agency for overthrowing the rule of capital and setting out to build a socialist, classless society was the working class? To answer, we need to understand how this discovery was derived from the most fundamental ideas in their whole philosophical and historical outlook. That outlook was formed through a critique of the highest achievements of philosophy and political economy in the bourgeois epoch. The greatness of those achievements (in the work of Hegel, Adam Smith and Ricardo) was in every case restricted, limited, because they could not go beyond the idea that the social relations formed on the basis of the rule of capital were the only possible ones, that these relations were 'rational', even natural, and that to consider going beyond them in practice or in thought was not in accordance with the laws of reason, and did not conform to an understanding of 'human nature'.

The 'human nature' they saw all around them – i.e. the characteristics of humans' behaviour formed under the rule of capital – they took to be characteristic of humans *as such*. Marx called this restricted and a-historical world view 'the outlook of political economy'[15] – which cannot go beyond the outlook of 'the isolated individual in civil society'.

The critique of this outlook by Marx and Engels led them to a development of concepts which revealed new truths about the reality, the limits and the *overcoming* of the rule of capital. It was on the basis of these concepts that they understood the revolutionary role of the proletariat.

First of all: the true 'subject' or active maker of the history of human societies is *labour*, the labour of men and women. Where capital rules, however, labour is *wage-labour*. This labour produces the means of life, of society, certainly, but it is initiated, controlled and dominated, and terminated by capital. 'In [the outlook of] political economy labour occurs only in the form of *activity as a source of livelihood*'.[16] Not only that; the worker's labour-power is a commodity bought by the capitalist, so that when it is activated, i.e. becomes actual labour, it belongs to the capitalist to use as he sees fit (i.e. profitable). The worker's work is alienated from him. Its life, its fate, depend on the movements and imperatives of investments and returns, and on the decisions taken in that world by the 'personifications of capital' who bought his labour-power. The social revolution (a 'second human revolution') is the reassertion of the primacy of the true subject, labour, labouring humanity.

Once we understand that capital is stored-up labour, the value accumulated by capital from that created by the labourers, it is clear that the worker is actually *ruled by his own product*, now in the hands of his class enemy. The social struggles engendered by this rule are *class struggles* between two structural antagonists – structural, in the decisive sense that their antagonism is not confined to this or that temporary or passing demand or reform, but is

---

[15] '*Society*, as it appears to the political economist, is *civil society* in which every individual is a totality of needs and only exists for the other person, as the other exists for him, insofar as each becomes a means for the other. The political economist reduces everything (just as does politics in its *Rights of Man*) to man, i.e. to the individual whom he strips of all determinateness so as to class him as capitalist or worker.' (Marx, *Economic and Philosophical Manuscripts of 1844*, in MECW, Vol.3, p. 317)

[16] Ibid, p. 241

essentially a matter of the ending or the continuation of the entire structure of capital's rule, economic, political-legal and ideological. This is what Marx meant when he said, 'The emancipation of the working class is the task of the working class itself.'

The political overthrow of the state power of capital is the *first step* in this 'overcoming' of capital's rule, this assertion of the self-rule of labouring humanity. Marx: 'The economic emancipation of the working class is the great end to which every political movement ought to be subordinate as a means.'

If Marx's outlook is taken to be some sort of 'economic determinism' (a distortion common to his critics and by some of his would-be followers), then the problem of 'agency' is surely insoluble. In reality, Marx's materialist conception of history is no economic determinism and is, on the contrary, essential to a proper understanding of the 'agency' problem.

For the 'social emancipation' of which Marx wrote there must be practice, organisation and consciousness developed by the working class itself, and there can be no question of some elite or enlightened force conducting the process. That is why Marx wrote (already in 1845 in *The German Ideology*) of the necessity of a 'mass communist consciousness'. For Marx and Engels the question is one of a *practical consciousness*, not simply a set of ideas. This practical consciousness must be a process of *mass* (practical) consciousness, that is, a conscious movement of the mass of the working class, in order to achieve the political overthrow of the capitalist state. But it is a great mistake to think that this is the end of the matter. For the ensuing task of the making of the new socialist/communist social order, a mass communist consciousness is clearly fundamental, because that making of the new order cannot be commanded from above, with retention of the old hierarchical division of labour and the division between mental and manual labour.

It is almost normal for Marxism to be criticised as determinist, as though Marx thought the development of capitalism's contradictions would inevitably result in the system's collapse and bring about the socialist revolution. All this, because, as we have already seen, Marx was alleged to be an economic determinist, i.e. that he thought economic development determined directly all historical (political, ideological, etc.) development. All too often, socialists have misunderstood Marx in similar fashion. Such a misinterpretation brings inconsistencies in theory and in practice, many times with tragic results. If the coming of the socialist revolution is inevitable, then how can the role of the working class be understood? Essentially, if ideas are determined by the economic base (i.e. by the social relations necessary to the role of capital) how can a socialist/communist consciousness possibly come into existence? The danger here is that somehow, magically, a self-appointed vanguard of some sort sees itself as escaping this determining of ideas and sets itself up as a 'leadership' for the working class, a class which is somehow inert but waiting to be led. Such a conviction leads to fruitless activity in efforts to oppose capitalism. Where a similar conviction takes hold in the period *after* the taking of state power, the results are tragic, as we have seen in the Soviet Union, China, North Korea and so on.

The text that is usually taken to support this widespread interpretation of Marxism as economic determinism is from Marx's preface to his *A Contribution to the Critique of Political Economy*, 1859:[17]

> In the social production of their existence, men inevitably enter into definite relations, which are independent of their will, namely relations of production appropriate to a given stage of development of their material forces of production. The totality of these relations of production constitutes the economic structure of society, the real foundation, on which arises a legal and political superstructure and to which correspond definite forms of social consciousness. The mode of production of material life conditions the general process of social, political and intellectual life. It is not the consciousness of men that determines their existence, but their social existence that determines their consciousness. At a certain stage of development, the material productive forces of society come into conflict with the existing relations of production or – this merely expresses the same thing in legal terms – with the property relations within the framework of

---

[17] Published in English by Lawrence and Wishart, 1971

which they have operated hitherto. From forms of development of the productive forces these relations turn into their fetters. Then begins an era of social revolution. The changes in the economic foundation lead sooner or later to the transformation of the whole immense superstructure. *In studying such transformations it is always necessary to distinguish between the material transformations of the economic conditions of production, which can be determined with the precision of natural science, and the legal, political, artistic or philosophic – in short, ideological forms **in which men become conscious of this conflict and fight it out**.'* (My emphasis, CS.)

There are distinctions here that are overlooked by critics and followers alike. Clearly the conflict between productive forces and outgrown social relations of production is not resolved *automatically*. On the contrary, it is *fought out* by men driven by 'ideological forms' in the sphere of politics, law, art, philosophy and so on. Since the character of these forms, as Marx clearly states, cannot be determined in the same way as can the economic foundations – 'it is always necessary to distinguish, etc.' – this 'ideological' part of the superstructure is relatively independent. That is to say, it is the sphere in which consciousness can break from the ruling ideas and practices (in the case of the movement to socialist revolution), break from 'the outlook of political economy', of 'the isolated individual in civil society', so that the working class can achieve class-consciousness, consciousness of being a 'class *for* itself', not simply 'in itself'.

Thus the 'forms in which men become conscious of this conflict and fight it out' are a manifestation of the unique fundamental character of human existence, the power of humans to engage with the rest of nature in such a way that they make their own history. *That* truly is 'human nature', as against the social character of the men and women formed by the rule of capital, as conceived by political economy and philosophy before Marx. These 'forms of consciousness' are not fixed structures confronting people but living processes of the working out of ideas and practices and the fight in which existing forms are challenged, modified, rendered obsolete or superseded.

Human society is the only part of nature which has gone beyond natural determination of its own 'nature' and discovered how to modify its environment and itself. This is the ultimate and continuing source of the whole business of 'agency', from the origins of tool-making to the proletarian revolution. That revolution, it cannot be too often repeated, is the assertion of what is distinctively human *against* the inhuman rule of capital, a rule which is the final manifestation of the rule *over* humans by that 'second nature', their own nature (production, culture) turned upside down in the history of class society.

Chapter 10
Defending the future

(a) The future under threat

Is it possible, in the course of organising to overthrow the capitalist class and end the rule of capital, to find ways of ensuring that the elementary conditions for communism prepared by capitalism itself are preserved and developed? It is obvious that this question has more importance than ever before, now that capital's mode of self-reproduction has become predominantly destructive of those basic cultural and natural conditions.

In my *Not Without a Storm*, I tried to say why any socialist movement that does not find ways now to protect and defend the natural and cultural conditions of the future socialist society is not worthy of the name. Here we confront a very difficult problem. Sociologists and others who write condescendingly about what they call 'working-class culture' forget that as an exploited class the proletariat has by definition been separated from cultural production and participation in mankind's cultural heritage. Individual members of the working class have always had to fight to overcome that separation. Yet the working-class movement must become constituted and its members conduct themselves in ways which already prepare us for what Marx called the 'human revolution', in opposition to capitalist barbarism. That will mean something very different from the hierarchical division of labour and often inhuman methods of organisation which have characterised the working-class movement until now.

Involved here is what István Mészáros calls 'the progressive acquisition of the alienated powers of decision-making by the structural antagonist of capital [i.e. the working class] who transforms in due course its members into the social body of freely associated producers.'

It has to be admitted that only with a new phase in the class struggle will we be in a position to be less vague than this, but it surely points the way forward. The great new means of communication (and it must be remembered that they already coincide to a great extent with means of production) delivered by information technology are central to these 'powers of decision-making' and to the whole material basis of the future socialist society. Not only must they be protected and defended, and their misuse fought at every turn, but they can also be in very definite ways appropriated, in the sense of using them to mobilise and organise against capital and to seek ways of building new initiatives which challenge capital's monopoly.

In this perspective, the *Communist Manifesto*'s reference to 'bourgeois intellectuals who go over to the proletariat' can take on a new significance, especially as scientists, writers and artists contemplate the threat posed by capital not only to their own work but also to the future of humanity and of the planet itself. Furthermore, because of past concessions forced upon the ruling class in the sphere of education and because of capital's ever-increasing need to have highly trained technicians, it is no longer only from the bourgeoisie that our 'intellectuals' will come. And a major consideration here is that millions of men and women who would a generation ago have been categorised as being in 'intellectual' occupations separate from the working class are everywhere being 'proletarianised'! Neither in their objective position vis-à-vis capital and the means of production nor in their consciousness can they continue to be described as 'middle-class'. What is certain is that sociologists of the 1960s and even later who wrote of 'bourgeoisification' of the working class were showing little foresight, to put it mildly.

(b) How to begin the defence?

In all this there are obviously new and extremely difficult problems. It is much easier to envisage ways of beginning to appropriate the 'means of communication', and to organise to exploit the vulnerability of transnational coordinated production to organised working-class action, than to see any way of encroaching on the actual means and process of material production. It should perhaps be added here that the situation of the working class in today's 'globalisation' positively demands new forms of organisation (in which the cooperation of scientists and those familiar with information technology will be essential).

This, for one thing, because the political/nation-state framework within which historically the working-class movement has organised and worked is of diminishing significance. There is no polity congruent with the economy of globalised capital, and rapidly diminishing possibility of 'representation' or political pressure and compromise. As for the state machine in the nation-states, it is not difficult to see that its basic functions will be laid bare when, as one Middle-East commentator nicely put it recently, we are witnessing in the advanced capitalist countries 'the withering away of the social welfare state'! What price reformism then? With anti-trade union legislation made and retained by 'Labour' as well as conservative parties, 'anti-terror' laws and identity cards and police surveillance, do we not have to return to and take heed of Engels' 'the state is an instrument of oppression of one class by another', *tout court*?

Denis Potter started writing with the perception that the new medium, television, held the promise of a 'common culture'. I see this as very like Marx's 'universal intercourse' plus highly developed productive forces, but alienated from, hostile to and invasive of humans. Potter had real insight into this.

Once again, Marx:

> The development of fixed capital indicates to what degree general social knowledge has become a direct force of production, and to what degree, hence, the conditions of the process of social life itself have come under the control of the general intellect and been transformed in accordance with it. (*Grundrisse*, p. 706)

As well as anticipating in a general way the significance of information technology, the last sentence suggests strongly that it is right to stress the importance of protecting and defending (and furthering?) these 'conditions of the process of social life' – now 'under the control of the general intellect' but with the resources of this 'general intellect' alienated from the direct producers in the hands of capital.

Given the new relationship between (globalised) capital and the nation-state, how is the great problem of appropriating the means of production to be addressed?

These means of production more and more coincide with the revolutionised means of communication and are transformed by this coinciding. The problem of appropriation/expropriation is no longer simply answered by 'take state power and expropriate'. Where state power can be taken, information technology will give that new state all sorts of possibilities not open, for example, to Soviet power after 1917. But how do you expropriate the transnational owners?

That question takes us back to the other interesting one. The electronic means of communication (computers, internet) are international and they are available not only to capital. Does not this 'knowledge revolution' open up the possibility, even before the conquest of state power, of our using these means of communication against capital, and as a resource for asserting counter-values?

Would not this be part of the necessity of defending from capital the essential cultural foundations of the future socialist society? And by doing so would we not be defending and protecting and developing these wonderful means of communication (and production) by using them for truly human purposes, against their use for exploitation?

As indicated above, exploring this question might give a whole new meaning to 'intellectuals who go over to the proletariat'. What Dennis Potter said about television is surely just as true of the internet. But more! Now, those who have been only consumers, receivers, readers of cultural products can be (and some already are) producers of them. What is available for consumption is another matter. Similarly, what resources (ideological, cultural awareness, education, skills) they have for producing is another matter. The internet is a means of production. The ends to be chosen and pursued – that is another question, just as Potter saw for television. For the most part, and for the masses, what is on television expresses the cultural degradation and depravity, or simply pap, which has been and still is relayed by all the media (some of it simply straight ideological propaganda, but done more efficiently, invasively and continuously than ever before). No doubt the content of the mental/cultural equipment of the great majority of those to whom the internet is available is formed largely by what they see on television. (It goes without saying that there are many independent producers and writers struggling – and sometimes succeeding against all odds – to make meaningful drama and enlightening documentaries.)

How can a beginning be made to take advantage of this new – and basically free – means of production, a means of production not in the hands only of capital? How can it be taken over, and to do what, in order to release creative energies, to challenge and counter the existing media diet and what it represents? How can it bring together those who can help to do this; to develop the internet as a means of organisation for those who are fighting in whatever ways to oppose the destructive order that is capitalism; to expose and organise against repression wherever it exists; to open the door to mankind's cultural heritage to those to whom it has always been closed? Will we not need a gateway or portal where all this can be brought together freely, to then be used, made available, organised, translated, distributed? This 'organisation' will be self-organisation, not a set of rules declared and enforced by some directing body. And it is not impossible.

Might we not have here, for the first time, a resource in which scientists, artists, designers, architects, town planners, educators, writers, poets, critics, philosophers, theoreticians, entertainers can begin to live together and work together with the mass of people from whom their work has been separated or who have been only consumers or receivers of that work? Could not that make possible the means for ordinary people to find expression for their latent talents, imagination, aspirations and thirst for knowledge? It could truly be an assertion, a real anticipation, of the values and potential creativity and freedom of the men and women of a cooperative social order of the future.

Obviously, the many struggles throughout the world against oppression, exploitation, war, deprivation and poverty, and the destruction of the planet's resources, are carried out in all sorts of ways independently of what is written about here concerning information technology and the internet. But there can be – and already is, in early forms – a bringing together of these struggles facilitated by the potential of the internet. Each will enrich all the others. It can be more than only a more efficient (and infinitely quicker!) form of organisation, coordination, networking (the best definition of organisation I ever heard was 'bringing good people together'). Be more than that, in what way? This question takes us back to that fundamental problem of our new millennium: the fact that the driving force of the productive basis of social life, the self-reproduction of capital, is now a destructive one.

Against capital's 'destructive self-reproduction', we are here insisting on the necessity of protecting, defending, and even developing, the basic conditions of the future positive society. At stake are the elementary natural bases of life, and also the advances in production and cultural life which have opened up the possibility and necessity of socialism. Among the latter are the conquests of science, information technology and the internet.

Therefore, when we discover and invent methods of using them in the ways suggested above, we will be beginning already to build, against the dehumanisation endemic to late capitalism, those truly human relations which will flower in a socialist society. In that society, human relations will rest soundly on an overcoming of the old, i.e. hierarchical and antagonistic, division of labour necessary to capitalism.

Now, we can begin work on how to use the internet as we have here argued above in ways which will already make a firm declaration – and even, when we are successful, a sound beginning of a change anticipating and positively starting to overcome the division of labour imposed on us by capital. We need a new Enlightenment – this time for everyone.

(c) 'Oppositional public space'

I suggest that these 'counter-culture' possibilities of use of the internet can be among the most positive and explosive elements of what

Oskar Negt has proposed as the building of an 'oppositional public space'.[18] If the problem of agency is discussed only in terms of the economic and political actions and theories that enter working-class consciousness, as we have tended to do in the past, then, Negt argues, new possibilities will be neglected. The energies and actions necessary for an effective and lasting challenge to the rule of capital will not be recognised, understood and engaged with, if we look only for how the working class can come to understand and exercise the revolutionary role attributed to it in theory.

Before exploring further these possibilities, it is useful briefly to glance at some alternative ideas of how the existing social order might be challenged and changed (I leave aside the surely discredited reformist, social-democratic programme of gradually introducing social welfare and democratic mechanisms in such a way as to overcome capitalism. This has had its history: the working-class parties which embraced it are no longer working-class parties, and it is becoming painfully obvious that as the structural crisis of capital unfolds, there is a clawing back of reformist gains, let alone no extension of them).

Against the encroaching power of the state over everyday life, there has been something of a revival of the idea of counterposing 'civil society' to the state. Essentially, the proposals flowing from this amount to an attempt to rally popular support for a democratisation of existing institutions. One of the strongest and most representative works in this category has the title *Reclaim the State*.[19] In this book Hilary Wainwright takes issue with the reactionary proposal discussed at European Union and World Trade Organisation level, which 'aims to force countries to open their public services to the private market'. Against this, she looks for a global challenge, with 'sustainable roots' planted by 'local processes with their own dynamics'. 'How', she asks, 'could such local power together with global action exert a pincer movement of democratic control over the national governments that have been both architects and accomplices of the new global power structure?'[20]

---

[18] Oskar Negt, *L'Espace Public Oppositionnel*, Payot, Paris, 2007
[19] Hilary Wainwright, *Reclaim the State: experiments in popular democracy*, Verso, 2003
[20] Ibid, p. 182

How, indeed. The movements in many parts of the world which she describes in her book are inspiring, and certainly such initiatives need to be brought together, coordinated, but I suggest that they will be frustrated so long as the aim of their coming together is that of exercising a measure of 'democratic control' over governments. Hilary Wainwright concludes that '... the whole rationale of participatory organisations is eventually to share decision-making with government, to exercise some control over the working of state institutions and to monitor the implementation of government's decisions.'[21]

The fundamental change in people's lives that is necessary goes beyond this 'rationale'. The power over our lives, and over the decisions of governments, is the power of capital. It is the imperatives of capital accumulation that determine the metabolism of social life everywhere, through whatever various and differing economic and political mediations they are imposed, and in 'advanced' as well as 'emerging' countries. As already indicated, a vital lesson of our history is that the end we need and wish to achieve must be held fast and built into every phase of the struggle and every form of organisation. That end is to replace the dehumanising power of capital through beginning to build a cooperative society of free and equal individuals, where labour will be devoted to the fulfilment of needs and not the accumulation of profit. The state, whatever the form of government, is the political instrument of capital's power. The aim must be to initiate the 'withering away of the state', not the sharing of power in the state with the political personifications of capital. Unless the 'participatory movements' in every country are orientated to this end, becoming loci of what Oskar Negt calls oppositional public space, they will reach a dead end. That is to say: they must take their place in the class struggle, part of the historically necessary unifying of all the struggles of the dispossessed of the world for the overthrow of their oppressor, capital. The potentially liberating form of this universal 'oppositional public space' is the internet.

Of equal interest, and subject to the same critical considerations, are the 'social centres' movement since the 1980s and the more political *centri sociali* in Milan. What follows is a

---

[21] Ibid. p. 183

brief summary of the informed and objective account published by Chatterton and Hodgkinson,[22] devoted to a critical analysis of the emergence of social centres and their role in both the development of autonomous politics and the growing urban resistance movement in the UK to the corporate takeover, enclosure and alienation of everyday life. These centres vary in origin and scope, but there is a common element of 'reclaiming private space and opening it up to the public as part of a conscious refusal and confrontation to neoliberalism and the enclosure of public space.' Instead of urban land being solely at the disposal of capital (and the 'Private Finance Initiatives' introduced by British governments have accentuated that monopoly), the aim is to use them to meet social needs.

The social centres, as well as posing a challenge to privatisation of public space, provide a focus for the organisation of solidarity with other forms of resistance and defence (solidarity with the Palestinian and Iranian peoples, opposition to the wars in Iraq and Afghanistan, environment campaigns, support for immigrant workers and asylum seekers, etc).

In this way they have the potential to be key links in the networks that will be necessary in the building of new, nationwide and international movements for fundamental social change. It is easy to see that internet access (free and universal) in these centres will play a major role. Chatterton and Hodgkinson present a balanced and objective view of the 'numerous challenges, tensions and even contradictions' in the 'everyday existence of social centres'. Where they are legalised, it will be necessary to guard against the erosion of their 'oppositional social space' character.

In stark contrast to these possibilities of oppositional public space is the increasingly common phenomenon of the building of private living spaces, gated, secured and policed estates (the word 'communities' is hardly appropriate). 'These micro fortifications now accommodate around four million US households and a thousand such developments across England.'[23] Here people look

---

[22] P. Chatterton & S. Hodgkinson, *Autonomy in the Cities? Reflections on the UK Social Centres Movement*, Leeds, 2006
[23] Rowland Atkinson, 'Prisoners by Choice', in *Le Monde Diplomatique* (English edition), June 2010. And see Thomas Sanchez, Robert Lang and

for a way of escaping the risks of insecurity and danger in urban life created by our 'overdeveloped' system and its social pathological results. But they embrace a 'solution' which defends their own place and relative privileges within that very 'overdeveloped' system and its values of individualism and self-interest. Their solution is itself one of those pathological results. Doris Lessing's *Memoirs of a Survivor* was truly prophetic. This search for private space is the very opposite of the 'oppositional public space' we are discussing.

All in all, there are possibilities here of the discovery of modes of opposing rather than of merely making use of 'public space', as that 'space' becomes increasingly privatised by capital, to become even more than it is today a world of sound-bites, flashed images, 'celebrities', 'winners and losers', and the pathetic 'reality TV'. There is potential for men and women to make their own decisions, to relate to each other freely and independent of any hierarchical or bureaucratic control.

This is not at all to say that such movements cannot degenerate and become dominated by new elites (as in the history of bureaucratisation of mutual organisations such as trade unions). The key issue will be the invention of methods of establishing collaboration and unity between these movements and achieving continuity, carrying forward the strengths, energies and lessons into further mobilisations. Undoubtedly it will only be in conditions of continuous/repeated crises that such continuity can be successfully fought for. It is easy to envisage ways in which partial and separate struggles of this kind merge into or develop into struggles at the level of class conflict. For example, it will be necessary to organise and find allies to defend such oppositional public space against state repression and the forces of 'law and order'. At that point, again, the development of opposition at the level of class struggle must come into play. And given the fact that in such movements for oppositional public space there is the

---

Dawn Dhavale, 'Security and Status', *Journal of Planning, Education and Research* 24, 2005, and Rowland Atkinson, Sarah Blandy, John Flint and Diane Lister, 'Gated Cities of Today?' *Town Planning Review* 76, 2005. Also Lieven de Cauter, *Capsular Civilization; on the City in the Age of Fear,* Nai Publishers, 2005

opportunity for the development of individuals' talents and imagination, and for the discovery of a social intercourse freed from the discipline and cultural programming of daily life in the world dominated by capital, then there can perhaps begin to be forged those human bonds and values which will be the foundation of a new social order.

Is this an idealised picture? There are good reasons not to think so. First; the overdevelopment of capital is certain to give rise to a multiplicity of problems which compel people to resist, to defend themselves, their living standards, their rights and their environment – their natural and their built environment. And secondly, to re-emphasise, there now exists a 'space' which, while it is used on a massive scale for capital's purposes, is free and available to all, a 'free space' with limitless promise for cultural expression, self-created social relationships, networks and organisation. It is the internet, a universal electronic 'space' available to millions and potentially to all. 'Oppositional' space in it can be occupied! Surely here is the quintessential 'oppositional public space' in the making. That is why big business firms in the United States are lobbying to do away with free access to the internet; and why in China, where regional resistance and democratic-rights movements have begun to coordinate their struggles by internet, the Stalinist-cum-capitalist rulers have found a way to consign one of the leading intellectuals who was working on this coordination to 18 years in a mental asylum.

The point was made in an earlier chapter about the problem posed by the competition between the immediate interests of workers in different countries. The building of international solidarity can be greatly facilitated by the use of electronic communication. Now we can see that Oskar Negt's work on 'oppositional public space' opens up a new dimension, a new significance for this weapon, the internet, as it does for the problem of the relation between the working-class movement and other social forces and issues, as well as for the vital question of how the movement for revolutionary change must and can become imbued with the values which will bind us together in a future, truly human society.

In this context, it will become more and more realistic and possible to put flesh and blood on the ambitious proposals of some socialists to initiate processes of equal exchange between producers (say, of engineering products) in Europe and North America and producers of raw materials and foodstuffs in Africa and Latin America. This could mean, even while capital remains the ruling power, the implantation, on both sides of the exchange, of the methods of production and control which must replace that power.

How could this happen? The deepening of the structural crisis of capital has consequences – particularly growing unemployment – which will force upon millions, and not only workers, the consciousness that truly radical alternatives must be found. And at the same time we can anticipate that the closure of factories and plants in one traditional industrial area after another, already begun, will provoke occupations and take-over of those plants, a circumstance in which these seemingly ambitious proposals will become eminently 'realistic'. This would indeed be 'oppositional public space', and in circumstances where one can envisage linked community actions. Such 'space' would have to be defended by all means, thus enhancing the prospect of movements at the class and political level, beyond merely local concerns. All this would have to be in situations where the bureaucratisation and opportunism of the trade unions was challenged, and the impotence of purely parliamentary 'opposition' recognised.

An afternote:

In the autumn of the year 2011, some months after this chapter was written, came a quite remarkable confirmation in practice of Oskar Negt's concept of 'oppositional public space', the anti-capitalist 'Occupy' actions which began in New York's Wall Street, spreading quickly to Seattle and other American cities and then to many other countries. One unemployed participant in the Frankfurt occupation told a reporter, 'I live alone, so it's nice to be with other people, planning the new world order.' In London, some hundreds of people camped in the City, under a large banner 'Capitalism is Crisis'. *The_Guardian*'s reporter wrote: '... they're not interested in making petty demands on a system they see as irreconcilably flawed,' and, very significantly in the present context: 'If anything, the camp itself is their demand, and their solution: the stab at an alternative society that at least aims to operate without hierarchy, and with full participatory democracy.' One young woman said: 'I feel like what I want to see is happening here, right now. A space to speak. A space to be heard.' An 18-year-old politics student: 'So the importance of this kind of space is in the way it brings together people to open up a dialogue about building an alternative.' A 31-year-old 'blogger': 'We're forming a space where people can come together and crystallise all of what we think. Out of this more concrete ideas can be formed.'

These occupiers of public space built their own 'institutions' in the camp: 'teams', dealing respectively with food, donations, education, relations with the police, legal matters, recycling, outreach, music, art and entertainment, relations with the media, etc. They established and maintained contact with occupations in other cities across the world. (All the above is taken from Patrick Kingsley's article 'Welcome to the Occupation' in *The Guardian*, 21 October, 2011.)

It is a safe bet that none of those interviewed had read Oskar Negt.

The 'Occupy' movement is of course part of an emerging reaction to the effects of 'globalisation' (the anodyne definition of the capital system's structural crisis). Alongside 'Occupy' come the general strikes in Greece against the Canute-like austerity measures taken to deal with the country's debt. Trade unions in New York, a century behind the 'occupiers'' use of electronic communication, marched in support, and a transit union refused police requests to transport occupiers arrested. The attempt to internationalise 'Occupy' shows a growing consciousness of the nature of the crisis and the opposition to its effects. The campers on Wall Street see a direct connection with the Tahrir Square demonstrators in Egypt. That 'Arab spring' was itself a manifestation of the same crisis, with the overthrow of a string of dictators who had served the big capitalist powers for two generations. The sudden conversion of European and American politicians to 'democracy' for North Africa (after Obama's initial reaction, 'Mubarak must stay') is touching, but along with it comes an emerging doctrine of 'humanitarian' military intervention to ensure that other dictatorial regimes are succeeded by amenable governments.

Other 'straws in the wind' indicating the political leaders' thrashing around for answers to the social problems arising from the apparent insolubility of the global economic crisis are the reactions of British cabinet ministers to what they see as a problem of unruly and criminal young people. Following the so-called 'riots' of 2011, Prime Minister Cameron engaged in a demagogic tirade about 'bad parenting, bad discipline, bad ethics' to initiate hundreds of kangaroo-court trials in which judges handed out absurdly harsh sentences. And Michael Gove, Minister for Education, wants to have history taught in the British imperial spirit, and favours new schools run on military lines by ex-officers. At the same time Liam Fox, Defence Secretary, takes on his ministerial missions a personal friend, who heads a bogus charity connected with extreme right-wing figures and arms manufacturers in the United States, and has to resign because he has broken the ministerial code, but feels confident in his right-with Tory support to make in the House of Commons an arrogant 'apology' that sounded more like a proclamation of candidature for future leadership of a right-wing coup d'etat.

Chapter 11
Ends and Means

(a) The necessity of a clear understanding of the end

'Agency' is the question of which social force will bring about the necessary fundamental social change, and by what means. The working-class and other movements in opposition to capitalism have until now been unable to make any decisive inroads into the power of capital, which despite their efforts has now grown to the point where its continuation threatens the very future existence of civilised life. A paramount reason for this ineffectiveness has been a failure to base opposition firmly on the understanding that the changes needed are indeed fundamental ones. Involved is not the reform of this or that aspect of the capitalist order, nor even only a revolution for the taking of state power, followed by the transfer of the means of production to state ownership. The forces for the necessary change will come together, self-organised, to conquer our future only when every phase of that coming together and self-organisation is informed, in theory and in practice, by an understanding of the magnitude of the transformation of life which is necessary.

From the time of his earliest writings, Marx had set out to discover the path to the realisation of the age-old dream of human freedom. 'The world has long possessed the dream of a thing that, made conscious, it would possess in reality.' 'His philosophical programme', writes Mészáros, was 'the complete emancipation of all human senses and attributes'. This meant the 'transcendence of labour's self-alienation', the question at the core of his life's work.

Only the struggle for this transcendence could open up the true meaning of human existence past, present and future, and give meaning to the old dreams of a future utopia. Walter Benjamin saw this task as to 'piece together what history has broken to bits.' (*The Arcades Project*, p. 944.)

Such a 'transcendence' will restore the truly human relation to the rest of nature, and at a level made possible by the advanced means of production and communication developed under capitalism.

The fact is that most socialists – in the name of Marxism – have until now treated Marx's most basic conceptions as some sort of youthful idealism, with no relevance to 'practical politics', something left behind by a mechanical idea of 'scientific socialism'.

It is interesting to glance at past ideas of utopia, both in writers like Fourier and Saint-Simon and in popular culture. Benjamin notes:

> One of the most remarkable features of the Fourierist utopia is that it never advocated the exploitation of nature by man, an idea that became widespread in the following period. Instead, in Fourier, technology appears as the spark that ignites the powder of nature ... . The later conception of man's exploitation of nature reflects the actual exploitation of man by the owners of the means of production. If the integration of the technological into social life failed, the fault lies in this exploitation.'(Ibid, p. 14.)

By 'reflects' here is meant more than in the usually understood sense of a mental reflection.

When the owner of the means of production buys the labour-power of the worker, he takes from that worker his truly 'human nature' – because the power to labour and produce is exactly what is distinctively human! The Marxists who think to develop a Marxist 'political economy', and stress only that labour-power is a commodity with value, price, etc., forget that what Marx wrote was a critique of political economy, an assertion of human self-emancipation against capitalist economy and its apologists. To put it briefly: our understanding of capitalist exploitation has often been too narrowly 'economic'.

'Too economic' here means too narrowly conceived as an 'economic' relation instead of how it should be conceived, i.e. as an 'anthropological' one, and that means conceiving it from the standpoint of human beings and their self-emancipation (*vide* Mészáros, *Marx's Theory of Alienation*).

In the same way, as Vasily Grossman's wonderful novel *Life and Fate* makes painfully clear, our understanding of Stalinism and the transition to socialism was, so to speak, 'too political'! Trotsky (see, for example his *The Revolution Betrayed*), and those of us who followed his criticism of 'socialism in one country' and the monstrous Stalinist regime, were certainly more correct than others in our political estimation. But – and it is a big 'but' – we fell painfully short of a properly 'anthropological' understanding; that is to say an understanding of the way in which more than a generation of men and women in the Soviet Union were subjected to a social and moral order profoundly destructive of their 'human nature'. Grossman tells us of acts of basic human kindness and sympathy, in face of all the baseness and horrors, which give us more for the future than all our hopes of a 'political revolution' which we saw as necessary against the Stalinist bureaucracy (let alone, of course, the dreams of the proponents of 'really existing socialism' and 'transition to communism' in the Soviet Union, or of 'cultural revolution' in China). Grossman writes:

> With Stalin's help, such revolutionary categories as dictatorship, terror, the rejection of bourgeois liberties – all those things which Lenin had considered temporary, transitory expedients – were transformed into the permanent basis of Soviet life, became its essence, and were absorbed into Russia's historical, thousand-year continuum of nonfreedom ....
>
> Stalin embodied a revolutionary of the Nechaev type, a person for whom any means at all were justified by the ends. But even Nechaev, of course, would have shuddered to see to what monstrous lengths Joseph Stalin developed the Nechaev principle. (pp. 226-7)

And further:

Terror and dictatorship swallowed up those who had created them. And the state, intended as the means to an end, turned out to be the end. The people who created it had conceived of it as a means to the realisation of their dreams. But it turned out that their dreams, their ideals, were merely a means, a tool, of the great and dread state. Instead of being a servant, as it was meant to be, the state had become a grim tyrant. (p. 193)

Lenin and his comrades did indeed think that the 1917 October revolution in Russia was the first step towards communism. But they knew that if Russia remained isolated, socialism/communism could not be achieved in Russia. The task, Lenin repeatedly asserted, was 'to hold out until the workers of the advanced countries come to our aid'. Why? Because the material and cultural conditions necessary for building socialism did not exist in Russia; only, they thought, on a world scale. It was Stalin and his supporters who invented (actually it was by no means an invention, but something put forward earlier by the German Social-Democrat Georg von Vollmar) the reactionary utopia of 'socialism in one country', against all the warnings of Lenin that Russia's backwardness and isolation, once the German revolution was betrayed and defeated, would lead to bureaucratic reaction. Leon Trotsky made a blistering critique of Stalin's project of 'socialism in a single country', a backward country at that. But he based his own position on his conviction that in the 'epoch of wars and revolutions' following the October Revolution of 1917, capitalism was a system in decay, and the conditions for socialist revolution were ripe on the world scale.
In this he was mistaken, but he was a thousand times right aboutd the Stalinist project of 'socialism in a single country' being a reactionary utopia at best, and his fight against Stalinism was unique, incomparable. Here again. And with the help of hindsight and of developments since Trotsky's assassination, we can learn from those of his conceptions which have proven to be mistaken.
Certainly it is easy to see how wrong he was when interviewed by Kingsley Martin of The New Statesman magazine in 1937 he said that in a few years time the Fourth International would be a mass force. But there are more serious and instructive aspects of Trotsky's ideas and programme which were

misconceived.

Central to Trotsky's perspective, and to his 'Transitional Programme', was the definition of the Soviet Union as a 'degenerated workers' state' (a confusion compounded by the Trotskyist movement's affirmation that the Eastern European countries coming under Stalinist domination after the Second World War were 'deformed workers' states'. I have already argued (above, and in my Not Without a Storm) that the polarity 'workers' state or bourgeois state' is no guide to the nature of the Soviet state (or, by extension, to the Eastern European post-WW2 and Chinese Maoist social systems and states). These states and their revolutionary origins proved in fact to be the only possible mechanism, in the imperialist period characterising the twentieth century, for taking backward countries on the road to national capitalism. As so often, men's actions, here revolutionary actions and aspirations, resulted in something that no one willed. Capitalism requires above all the creation of a propertyless and disciplined working class, and these so-called 'workers' states' proved to be the instruments for creating such a class.

At the root of Trotsky's idea of the Soviet Union as a (degenerated) workers' state is his insistence, in everything he wrote on 'the class nature of the Soviet state', that the class nature of a state depends first and foremost, and fundamentally, on the form of property in the means of production in the country. Some examples, all taken from Trotsky's writings in the 1930s:

'The class character of the state is determined by its relation to the forms of property in the means of production.'

'The USSR is only a partial and mutilated expression of a backward and isolated workers' state.'

'The proletariat of the USSR is the ruling class in a backward country where there is still a lack of the most vital necessities of life.'

'One can with full justification say that the proletariat, ruling in one backward and isolated country, still remains an oppressed class. The source of oppression is world imperialism; the mechanism of transmission – the bureaucracy.'

'...the bureaucracy has expropriated the proletariat politically in order to guard its social conquests with its own methods... So long as the forms of property that have been created by the October Revolution are not overthrown, the proletariat remains the ruling class.'

'... despite monstrous bureaucratic degeneration, the Soviet state still remains the historical instrument of the working class insofar as it assures the development of economy and culture on the basis of nationalised means of production and, by virtue of this, prepares the conditions for a genuine emancipation of the toilers through the liquidation of the bureaucracy and of social inequality.'

Actually, corresponding more closely to the historical reality is the formulation he takes from Lenin: 'a bourgeois state without the bourgeoisie.' Lenin was here acknowledging that the revolution in a backward country left the new state with no alternative to using 'bourgeois right' in the distribution of life's necessities.

Lenin devoted one of his best-known works to the question of The State and Revolution, of which, incidentally, Trotsky was critical (see his The Revolution Betrayed). Lenin's definition of the state and its class character (following that of Marx and Engels) is very different from Trotsky's. For him the nature of the state is not simply, or in the first place, a matter of property forms in the means of production. Thus he writes: 'According to Marx, the state is an organ of class rule, an organ for the oppression of one class by another...' and 'What does this (state) power mainly consist of? It consists of special bodies of armed men having prisons, etc., at their command.' He then refers to Marx's characterisation of the 1871 Paris Commune as the dictatorship of the proletariat (a characterisation, incidentally, criticised by Trotsky), and recalls the Communist Manifesto's '... highly interesting definition of the state, which is also one of the "forgotten words" of Marxism: "the state, i.e., the proletariat organized as the ruling class."'

On this definition, from which neither Marx, Engels nor Lenin ever departed, it is surely impossible to see Stalin's Russia, or Mao's China, as a workers' state. There, 'special bodies of armed men', prisons, etc., were used systematically and brutally to oppress the working class'. We can adapt the expression 'bourgeois state without the bourgeoisie' as follows. The Soviet state was a machine for the oppression of the working class in a way not seen before in history. It was the necessary instrument (completely contrary to the intentions and methods of those who made the October revolution), given the economic and political conditions of the imperialist stage of capitalist development, for the growth and the disciplining of a propertyless working class, the basic resource for the emergence of capitalism in a backward country.

In other words, the result of the Stalinist project, repeated in its own way in Mao's China, turned out to be the creation, in a quite new and unintended way, of the conditions for the formation of an independent capitalist nation-state. In the closing years of the twentieth century, the state-bureaucrat rulers of Russia and China were transformed overnight into ruling capitalist classes. In the 'globalised' capitalist 'free world' in which these nation-states emerged after the collapse of the Soviet Union in 1989-90, there was no room for a 'democratic revolution' like those which had accompanied the transition to capitalism in Europe at the end of the feudal era, (any more than the 'democracy' which some pundits in America and Europe seem to have persuaded statesmen would come with the restoration of capitalism). Instead these countries have an authoritarian and parasitic, even mafia-like ruling class.

The result of the Stalinist project, repeated in its own way in Mao's China, turned out to be the creation, in a quite new and unintended way, of the conditions for the formation of an independent capitalist nation-state. In the closing years of the twentieth century, the state-bureaucrat rulers of Russia and China were transformed overnight into ruling capitalist classes. In the 'globalised' capitalist 'free world' in which these nation-states emerged after the collapse of the Soviet Union in 1989-90, there was no room for a 'democratic revolution' like those which had accompanied the transition to capitalism in Europe at the end of the feudal era, (any more than the 'democracy' which some pundits in America and Europe seem to have persuaded statesmen would come with the restoration of capitalism). Instead these countries have an authoritarian and parasitic, even mafia-like ruling class.

(b) Against 'the end justifies the means'

It is essential that 'the means themselves are absolutely imbued with the very nature of the end' (Ferdinand Lassalle).
First it has to be said that the end itself must be justified.
Clearly, the maxim that 'the end justifies the means' is incompatible with Marx's 'philosophical programme' of 'the complete emancipation of all human senses and attributes' and with 'the transcendence of labour's self-alienation' (above). Equally it is incompatible with an understanding that the emancipation of the working class is the task of the working class itself.
Here it is worth quoting from the Provisional Rules of the First International:

Considering:

... That the emancipation of the working class must be conquered by the working classes themselves: that the struggle for the emancipation of the working classes means not a struggle for class privileges and monopolies, but for equal rights and duties, and the abolition of all class rule

... that the economical emancipation of the working class is... the great end to which every political movement ought to be subordinate as a means...

(Clearly, this 'end' becomes, in the wider context of 'emancipation of all human senses and attributes', a means – one example of a general rule for the relation between means and ends.)
Now, this 'end', 'abolition of class rule', is not reached with the political revolution to overthrow the capitalist ruling class. This revolution initiates the long and complex process in which the producers in common themselves create the conditions of their 'economical emancipation', which means equal rights and duties of all, the social revolution, what Marx called the human

revolution. The political revolution is the climax of 'every political movement', and is subordinate as a means to this long process of self-emancipation.

Certainly the political revolution is an end as well as a means to the fundamental end. But is a gross mistake to work politically as if any means is justified by the necessity of that revolution. All means, all methods, all forms of work and organisation, all relationships in the political movement and between the movement and the working class as a whole, must be consistent with the great end to which every political movement, including that movement's climax, the revolution, must be subordinate. Such a conception must be held fast at every phase of the transitional period opened up by the revolution – a maxim in the sharpest possible contrast to the Stalinist regime in the Soviet Union.

The International's Rules continue:

> [We] declare that this International and all societies and individuals adhering to it, will acknowledge truth, justice and morality, as the basis of their conduct towards each other, and towards all men, without regard to colour, creed, or nationality.

In the Inaugural Address of the International, we find: '... numbers [of the proletariat] weigh only in the balance, if united by combination and led by knowledge.' This seems very elementary, but is it not interesting for two reasons?

1. The numbers of the proletariat (against all the dire predictions of the sociologists) are far, far greater than in 1861, and they are in every country on the globe. This poses the great question of their 'combination/organisation' in confronting and combating capital on the global arena.
2. 'Knowledge' – not a worked-out 'revolutionary consciousness' delivered to the working class by a self-appointed vanguard. Elsewhere in these documents, Marx refers to 'the most enlightened members of the

working class' etc. and it is sure he thinks it is they who are the 'vanguard'.

Here we should re-emphasise (see above, in the chapter 'Defending the Future') that the Manifesto's 'bourgeois intellectuals going over to the proletariat' needs reflection. Because of the concessions won by past bitter struggles, education and the possibility of being 'intellectuals' are there for the working class. Furthermore, millions of people whose occupations may once have separated them from the proletariat are now in the position of proletarians in relation to capital (information technology has a massive impact on both of these).[24]

Similarly, on questions of consciousness and leadership, we should be thinking about Lenin's criticism of spontaneity and its limits (*What is to be Done*) in the light of the International's declaration on 'Cooperative Labour':

> It is the business of the International Working Men's Association to combine and generalise the spontaneous movements of the working class, but not to dictate or impose any doctrinary system whatever.

This conception was lost during the dominance of Stalinism in the working-class and revolutionary movements of the twentieth century, reflected in the distortions of 'democratic centralism' even in anti-Stalinist groups. As the collapse of the Soviet Union and Stalinism approached in the 1980s, a French comrade, Raoul, was able to speak of 'the end of the age of the commissar'. Ideas of what constituted leadership and the qualities of a 'leader' were common in almost all the groups and parties trying to be communist. Two correctives would have been salutary. Raoul, a highly respected Trotskyist, wrote: 'The role of a leader is to be listened to and respected, not feared'(in Pierre Broue, *Raoul*). The novelist Balzac, an amazingly wise social commentator, wrote, 'To lead a party is it not necessary to be in concordance with its ideas?' (*La Duchesse de Langeais*.)

---

[24] See especially David Hookes' paper, 'The information proletariat in the era of globalisation': http://hometown.aol.co.uk/davehookes/Moscow3.pdf.

Certainly the Stalinist regime in the Soviet Union, with its totalitarian control and ruthlessness, was the extreme example of the deadly consequences of proceeding on the axiom 'the end justifies the means'. Replying to those apologists for Stalinism who said, 'You can't make an omelette without breaking eggs', George Orwell asked: 'Where's the omelette?' Quite so; not *any* means will produce the desired end. In the fight for a new world, the types of organisation, tactics and leadership adopted must have a content which is not in contradiction to the end to which we aspire: the liberation of men and women and of all their potential from all forms of domination and exploitation. The fundamental objective, freedom, must not be negated in the means adopted to attain it. As Antonio Gramsci expressed it: 'For leaders, the premise is fundamental: do we want there always to be governed and governing, or, on the contrary, do we want to create conditions in which the necessity of this division disappears?'[25]

In the history of socialist movements, it is not only the Stalinist dictatorship which has in practice contradicted this principle. The fact is that socialist politics will have to be renewed by subjecting to radical criticism some ideas and practices upon which parties and groups other than Stalinist ones, including avowedly anti-Stalinist (e.g. Trotskyist) organisations, have based their work. Such a critique will show there has been a failure to reject decisively the notion that 'the end justifies the means'. This failure has been compounded by the persistent tendency to substitute 'the party' for the working class as the agent of the revolution. But by showing how these principles have been ignored or distorted, we do not yet approach a positive solution to our main problem, namely: what are the means which will indeed lead towards the desired end, a society of free men and women? Knowing the objective and striving to ensure that our actions are always consistent with it, does not tell us what means will lead to that end, what social force can initiate and carry through the change. That is to say: we cannot deduce from our consciousness of the end the means to achieve it.

As against a purely utopian dream of a future social order, we know that the elementary material or objective conditions for that

---

[25] Antonio Gramsci, *Selections from the Prison Notebooks*, Lawrence & Wishart, 1971

future society (greatly advanced productive forces, 'universal intercourse') are prepared by the existing system. The great problem is: how are the means to effect the necessary transformation, a truly revolutionary change, to emerge from those same existing conditions? Socialists have based their answer, their politics, on Marx's conclusion that it is the working class created by and essential to capitalism, that is driven to challenge and overthrow the capitalist system. In other parts of the present work, we address questions raised by the changed composition and role of the working class, but at this stage of the discussion we must occupy ourselves with a fundamental issue that, of the class-consciousness of the working class.

(c) Class-consciousness: class and party

All too often this has not even been seen as a problem, as when professed Marxists engage in politics as if the working class by its very nature is socialist, or, just as mistaken a notion, predisposed to accept a socialist class-consciousness delivered to it ready-made by a self-appointed 'vanguard'. I leave aside the naïve notion that education and propaganda alone will convince the working class that they must make a socialist revolution. In all these cases there is complete neglect of a simple truth: it is necessary for socialists to learn as well as to teach; socialist theory must be developed, not simply delivered.

In point of fact, very difficult theoretical questions are involved. A thoroughly critical reappraisal of these matters may appear too abstract, and a digression, but without it we cannot get any farther with the old problem of 'ends and means'. Until recently, the outstanding work on this question was *History and Class-consciousness*, written by the Marxist, Georg Lukács.[26] We now have an exhaustive critique of that work by István Mészáros, a fellow-countryman and former pupil and collaborator of Lukács.[27] Most of what follows here is informed by that critique.

---

[26] Georg Lukács, *History and Class-consciousness*, Merlin Press, 1971
[27] István Mészáros, *Beyond Capital*, esp. part 2

Lukács sees the working class as having a 'reified' consciousness resulting from its alienation and ideological domination by capital. In order to be able to execute its historical revolutionary role, it must have a consciousness of that role, something possible only on the basis of Marx's theories. Only a party, already having this consciousness, can bring it to the class. Mészáros concentrates his criticism on this notion of the working class becoming conscious of its revolutionary role through 'the work of consciousness on consciousness'. It is a notion which leads Lukács to ignore the necessary 'material mediations', i.e. the struggles and experiences through which the working class can become a 'class for itself' and not just a 'class in itself'. The dangers here (especially with hindsight) are striking. Lukács sees the party as 'the organised incarnation of proletarian class-consciousness', its 'conscious collective will', 'the concrete mediation between man and history'.

In very crude and distorted ways, this basic flaw in Lukács' theory has had practical manifestation in the history of Communist Parties, but also of the groups that have followed Trotsky in trying to build revolutionary parties in opposition to Stalinism. A fundamental error here was, and is still, to see revolutionary class-consciousness (consciousness of the necessity of revolution) as an already known entity, incarnated in the form of a 'vanguard' party for the working class, not of the working class, and to be delivered, so to speak, to the class. To this end, Lenin's booklet *What is to be Done* (1902) is called up, and in particular his dictum that the working class can spontaneously attain only a 'trade union consciousness', not a revolutionary, political one. Consequently, this revolutionary consciousness, the product of bourgeois intellectuals, has to be 'brought' to the working class, 'from the outside', by a revolutionary party.[28]

It is easy to see that elitism (the party as elite) can be the outcome of such a conception. Should a party adhering to it come to hold the reins of state power, the consequences could under

---

[28] To what extent Lenin's formulations about the vanguard party and class-consciousness may have been exaggerated because of the necessity of a conspiratorial organisation and by the demands of an inner-party polemic against 'worship of spontaneity' is still a controversial matter

some circumstances be lethal. Such a conclusion is not entirely hypothetical; the example of state terror in Stalin's Soviet Union is there for all to see. Is it any wonder that when members of the French Trotskyist group, the OCI (Organisation Communiste Internationaliste), were expelled for 'disloyalty to the party', they shuddered to think what penalty they would have paid for the same 'crime' had their party been in power?[29]

The idea of *partiinost* (effectively, loyalty to the party above all else) easily becomes a self-censorship and submission to the authority of leaders, Again an example from the French OCI: Raoul, principled critic and opponent of the authoritarian leadership of Pierre Lambert, had as his closest ally one François Demassot. When it came to confronting Lambert with their opposition, Demassot retreated, with a note to Raoul: 'I have chosen the party'. Raoul's comment was deadly accurate: 'That is Stalinism'.

The evolution of anti-Stalinist left/revolutionary groups is thus just as relevant to the study of the dangers of elitist conceptions of revolutionary class-consciousness as is the history of Stalinism (without of course implying in any way that the two are identical in their results and historical significance). When Trotsky's 'Bolshevik-Leninist' opposition to Stalinism was still organising in the Soviet Union (1928-29), the support it received in the working class was effectively squandered because Trotsky and his leading comrades clung to the idea that the task was only to change the policies and leadership of the Bolshevik Party and thus reform the so-called workers' state. They ignored critics in their own ranks who saw the necessity to go with the many workers who knew that this state was now oppressing them and was their enemy.[30] Trotsky's heroic and principled opposition to Stalinism (for which he paid with his life) should not blind us to the fact that his Fourth International can now be seen to have had a grave theoretical weakness in its programmatic base. The degeneration and betrayals of the Stalinist bureaucracy's Comintern resulted in defeats in Germany and China, and soon Spain. Trotsky, in his *The*

---

[29] Evidence from members of the *Carré Rouge* group.
[30] See Alexei Gusev, 'The "Bolshevik Leninist" Opposition and the working class, 1928-1929', in *A Dream Deferred: new studies in Russian and Soviet labour history*, Bern, 2008

Death Agony of Capitalism and the Tasks of the Fourth International; Transitional Programme, concluded from these experiences, and from the supposition that capitalism was in its period of decay, that 'the crisis of humanity is reduced to the crisis of working-class revolutionary leadership'.

It has to be admitted that the organisational and political practice of would-be revolutionary from parties and groups has consequently since then tended always to assume that the objective conditions for social revolution, and even the readiness for battle of the working class, can be taken for granted, leaving only one task to be completed – 'the building of the revolutionary party, the alternative leadership'. Such organisations took on the character of sects, with their isolation, with few exceptions, from the everyday life and struggles of ordinary people, and their doctrinaire splits. These tiny groups copied the structure of 'central committees', 'political bureaux' and 'control commissions' from the big parties of the Comintern, with the 'leadership' imposing a deadly conformism and burden of sacrifices of the time and financial resources of their members. Mike Davis hit the nail on the head, commenting on the left's obsession 'that the working class of the 30s and 40s, like the characters in a Clifford Odets play, were there waiting, in raw militancy and spontaneous class instinct, for the "correct" revolutionary line.'[31]

The reality is that capital's capacity for survival and further expansionary growth was by no means exhausted in the 1930s, when Trotsky wrote his programme, and the conditions and experience of working-class life were changing in decisive ways not to be comprehended by simply asserting that the world had entered 'the epoch of wars and revolutions'. There will be dogmatic self-styled adherents of Trotsky and Bolshevism who will denounce what I have just written as 'revisionism'. So be it: we must revise what needs to be revised.

If these conceptions of leadership, party and class-consciousness have indeed been put to the test of history and found to have failed, what then are the elements of a positive overcoming of the problem?

---

[31] Mike Davis, *Prisoners of the American Dream*, Verso, 2000, p. 53

Against the notion of a class-consciousness imputed to the working class and brought to it by a 'leadership' (party) holding the correct ideas, it is first of all necessary to insist on two basic considerations. Firstly; all who come into the struggles of the working class (and others who come into conflict with capital and its depredations) will need to rely not on the authoritative dictates of leaders but, in the first place, on the developing consciousness of the kind of society which is now possible and to which we aspire. This will come about in the course of experience of what the present social order is not, its denial of human needs and aspirations, so that in furthering opposition to it we are already building the values we know must prevail in the new society. Such a consciousness is, to repeat, not a ready-made one, known to the vanguard in advance, to be delivered to the working class. It must develop not only as a consciousness of the need to conquer state power in a political revolution, but as a consciousness of the need to overcome every way in which the order imposed by capital exploits, oppresses, degrades and dehumanises those dominated by it. Such consciousness is not known in advance by a theory-armed minority; it will be a 'practical consciousness' learned and built in the experience of those who come into conflict with the rule of capital.

At this point we can return to the basic errors in Lukács' conception of class-consciousness. As against his idea of just an ideological process of a vanguard imparting to the working class an already known revolutionary consciousness ('the work of consciousness on consciousness', the overcoming of false consciousness), the working class can achieve the consciousness necessary to overcome capital's rule only practically, in the course of discovering in practice, in struggle (essentially, the class struggle), the ways in which capital makes impossible a truly human existence. Thus what is necessary is to discover (not presuppose) and prepare for the 'material mediations' (forms of struggle) through which political consciousness will develop.

(d) A working class 'stitched up'

For this, we must understand that the working class is held back from knowing its real interests as a class, controlled, not only ideologically.

Held back? Perhaps 'stitched up' is more appropriate. I mean to say that this has happened to the working class in the older, 'advanced', overdeveloped capitalist countries in many, very material ways. In addition to the oppressive discipline of wage-labour, which has always been there, there are other factors. Politically, the working class is disenfranchised, its traditional parties having gone over openly to the side of capital. Socially and financially, workers and their families are weighed down by debt obligations, reliance on state benefits and payment for utilities provided by the state. The state itself makes ever-increasing inroads into the affairs of every citizen, as well as effecting legislation to increase its repressive powers. Ideologically, capitalist control of the mass media works to isolate the individual as a self-interested spectator, militating against any form of solidarity.

To make this point is even more important and urgent than when Lukács was writing (around 1920), for the following reason. It is easy to say that Marx's 'Workers of the world, unite! You have nothing to lose but your chains' can no longer be understood in exactly the same sense as when it was written, in 1847-8. Today, workers in the overdeveloped countries see themselves as having much more to lose. Many of them possess, or are purchasing, goods which once were luxuries (homes of their own, cars, holidays abroad, etc)). They have financial obligations which would cripple them even further than they already do if their incomes failed or declined. They have inherited a system of state benefits (pensions, etc) which could in the past be gained because of the exploitation of colonial peoples. But are not these gains also, in a more fundamental sense, 'chains', in that they put a brake on any sustained militant action, solidarity and organisation aimed at ending their subordinate and exploited status as a class?

These ties to the existing system are in this way an obstacle to class-consciousness, just as are the political and social factors already discussed above (it is for this reason that I used the colloquial term 'stitched up', which seems to me worthy of promotion to the ranks of theoretical language). Workers in Europe and America are certainly not in the same position of having 'nothing to lose but their chains' as are the working people of Africa, Asia and Latin America, where poverty, infant mortality and lack of the most elementary conditions of a decent life affect billions. In Africa, more than 200 million children are employed by capitalist firms as workers. Millions live on less than two dollars a day. In 'independent' Kenya's capital, Nairobi, is the Kibera slum, where 700,000 people live, 3,000 per hectare. 70 per cent of Africa's 760 million people live in slums. Only 20 per cent of the urban population have access to drinking water, and only 10 per cent to a sewage system.

At both ends of this spectrum (and for a more nearly complete picture of today's working class we would have to consider the billions of people in the countries emerging from Stalinist rule such as China, now numerically the most important workforce in capitalism) there clearly are very material conditions which must be confronted and overcome in struggles which go far beyond the merely ideological battle seen as decisive by Lukács. According to him, the 'ideological crisis' of the proletariat must be resolved 'before a practical solution to the world's economic crisis can be found'. This differs little if at all from Trotsky's line some 20 years later: 'The crisis of humanity is reduced to the crisis of revolutionary working-class leadership'. Trotsky and his followers were right to point to the decisiveness of betrayals and defeats of the working class, but failed to recognise the scope give by those defeats for capitalism's renewed phases of expansion. Lukács similarly never takes into account the way in which, through reformist policies and governments and welfare state measures as well as international agreements, capitalism would be able to postpone the manifestations of its contradictions and periodic crises.

We can conclude that the achievement of the consciousness necessary for achieving a fundamental change is a process, developing unevenly in struggle, as, for example, coming to recognise that if a particular campaign or protest or strike or occupation remains isolated (spatially and/or temporally) it will be dissipated or defeated (the 1984-5 British miners' strike) or will degenerate (the Russian and Chinese revolutions). We should not here be misled into a kind of gradualism. There cannot be the slightest doubt that only in a political and economic crisis of the most severe kind, when none of the most basic requirements and demands of people simply can be met, and their resistance is met by attempts at repression, could the lessons learned in earlier struggles come together and inform a rapidly growing unity for resolute action (one recalls Lenin's definition of a revolutionary situation, a situation where the people cannot live in the old way and the ruling class cannot rule in the old way). Until that day, only a stubborn and continuous struggle to hold fast to consciousness of the overall objective in the course of all partial struggles can prevent the partial movements of resistance from congealing into inertia and disillusion, with the re-emergence of self-appointed hierarchies and sects.

Here it is worth repeating that it would be a mistake to think and act as though only directly political and economic conflicts will be involved in the development of a mass movement for fundamental change, and certainly a mistake to think that all demands and movements building up to it will be explicitly socialist. In the last analysis, everything will depend on whether the existing system can partially satisfy or divert people's demands. These demands will be very diverse in their content and social origin, because the material means for educated, creative individuality with the potential of universality have been developed within capital's contradictory evolution, yet capital itself stands in the way of free access to them. Not only those who have read Marx on the nature of capitalist exploitation will come to see this, and it is the basis for leaps in consciousness of many kinds.

Everything is done – from the alienating labour process and manipulation of the patterns of material and cultural consumption by the mass media's imposition of ready-made responses and aspirations, to the fake 'democracy' of parliamentary politics – to confine the vision and powers of resistance of ordinary people to merely their immediate problems and experiences. Here the ideological struggle, aiming to overcome the prison of the immediate, certainly has its importance. It must be conducted consistently, analysing and dissecting every development, as an integral part of the many and varied social movements which will inevitably grow. But, to repeat, the 'working of consciousness upon consciousness' cannot be enough. There must be conditions in the class struggle itself in which a 'practical consciousness' (Marx) of the necessity of revolution is forged.

As an epilogue, not meant to be frivolous, to this chapter, this passage from Peter Carey's wonderful *True History of the Kelly Gang*:

Joe Byrne were the scholar amongst us many is the poem he wrote and the song he sang but Joe were inclined to be quiet in his opinion unless riled. By contrast you would think Steve Hart were a Professor to hear him on the state of Ireland blah blah blah rattling off the names of his heroes Robert Emmett and Thomas Meagher and Smith O'Brien he never seen them men but he were like a girl living in Romances and Histories always thinking of a braver better time.

Joe and me occupied the waking world we knew our hard circumstances was made by Whitty and Mc Bean who picked the eyes out of the country with the connivance of the politicians and police. Against their force all this queer boy's daydreaming were no defence at all his Irish martyrs couldn't get us decent land not even remove our cows from Oxley Pound. The following morning I told him he had better leave. (QPD in association with Faber & Faber, 2000)

Chapter 12
Utopias, and a Way Forward?

(a) Some past utopias

In popular culture, there is a centuries-long tradition of celebrating a future utopia (I leave aside mythological utopias like the classical Greek 'golden age' and literary utopias like that of Sir Thomas More). In what is written above, we have tried to explore the conditions for going beyond class society. We should enjoy and be strengthened by the utopian aspirations of our forefathers, as well as by their struggles.

Followers of Saint-Simon wrote:

> Yes, when all the world from Paris to China
> Pays heed to your doctrine, O divine Saint-Simon,
> The glorious Golden Age will be reborn.
> Rivers will flow with chocolate and tea,
> Sheep roasted whole will frisk on the plain,
> And sautéed pike will swim in the Seine.
> Fricasséed spinach will grow on the ground,
> Garnished with crushed fried croutons;
> The trees will bring forth apple compôtes,
> And farmers will harvest boots and coats.
> It will snow wine, it will rain chickens,
> And ducks cooked with turnips will fall from the sky.
> (Cited in Benjamin, *The Arcades Project*)

This vision no doubt derives from the 'Land of Cockayne' and the millenarian movements of medieval Provence. It is echoed many times, as in the familiar 'Big Rock Candy Mountain'. Here is one of the many versions:

> One evening as the sun went down
> And the jungle fires were burning,
> Down the track came a hobo hiking,
> He said, 'Boys, I'm not turning
> I'm heading for a land that's far away
> Beside the crystal fountain.
> I'll see you all this coming fall
> In the Big Rock Candy Mountain.
> Chorus:
> Oh the buzzin' of the bees
> In the cigarette trees
> Near the soda water fountain
> At the lemonade springs
> Where the bluebird sings
> On the Big Rock Candy mountain
> In the Big Rock Candy Mountain,
> It's a land that's fair and bright,
> The handouts grow on bushes
> And you sleep out every night.
> The boxcars all are empty
> And the sun shines every day
> I'm bound to go
> Where there ain't no snow
> Where the sleet don't fall
> And the winds don't blow
> In the Big Rock Candy Mountain.
> (Chorus)
> In the Big Rock Candy Mountain
> You never change your socks
> And little streams of alkyhol
> Come trickling down the rocks.
> O the shacks all have to tip their hats.
> And the railway bulls are blind.
> There's a lake of stew
> And gingerale too.
> And you can paddle all around it in a big canoe.

In the Big Rock Candy Mountain
(Chorus)
In the Big Rock Candy Mountain.
The cops have wooden legs.
The bulldogs all have rubber teeth
And the hens lay soft-boiled eggs.
The farmer's trees are full of fruit
And the barns are full of hay.
I'm bound to go Where there ain't no snow
Where the sleet don't fall
And the wind don't blow
In the Big Rock Candy Mountain.
(Chorus)
In the Big Rock Candy Mountain
The jails are made of tin.
You can slip right out again,
As soon as they put you in.
There ain't no short-handled shovels,
No axes, saws nor picks,
I'm bound to stay
Where you sleep all day,
Where they hung the jerk
That invented work
In the Big Rock Candy Mountain.

And in my childhood days I listened to the stern ladies of a Methodist chapel in a Durham mining village enthusiastically singing the hymn, 'There is a happy land', written by Andrew Young in 1838:

There is a happy land, far, far away,
Where saints in glory stand, bright, bright as day,
Oh, how they sweetly sing, worthy is our Saviour King,
Loud let His praises ring, praise, praise for aye.
Come to that happy land, come, come away;
Why will ye doubting stand, why still delay?
Oh, we shall happy be, when from sin and sorrow free,
Lord, we shall live with Thee, blest, blest for aye.
Bright, in that happy land, beams every eye;
Kept by a Father's hand, love cannot die.

Oh, then to glory run; be a crown and kingdom won;
And, bright, above the sun, we reign for aye.

At home and on the street it went to the same tune and with equal gusto, but slightly differently:

There is a happy land far, far away.
Where little piggies run, all through the day.
Oh you should see them run, When they see the butcher come.
Three slices off their bum, Three times a day.

(b) Is our vision of the future utopian? And Guadeloupe

We have argued that the necessary movement to overcome the now destructive work of capital must hold fast at all times and in all forms of organisation to the human content of a future truly human society. This 'holding fast' will not be in conflict with past popular ideas of 'utopia'.

It is already part of the tradition of working-class movements, now largely hidden by the pragmatic adaptation to capital by those who leaders and doctrines which have dominated the working class and radical movement. Of the working-class fighters he admired, Paul Mason has written: 'They fought, as was said of Jim Larkin, "for the flowers in the vase as well as the loaf of bread on the table."'[32] And Louise Michel, heroine of the Paris Commune, said that 'she had declared a hundred times that everyone should take part in the banquet of life.' She also understood that it is to that future 'banquet' that every struggle, even in defeat, has meaning only in relation to the end to be achieved: 'The Commune could only be brave, and it was. And in dying, it opened wide the door to the future. That was its destiny.'[33]

---

[32] Paul Mason, *Live Working or Die Fighting: how the working class went global*, Verso, 2008, p. 283
[33] Cited in ibid, pp. 60 and 76

There is a simple difference between the utopias of the past and some aspirations that may be called utopian in our own day. The fact is that the objective conditions of a universal truly human existence did not exist until now, when the unprecedented advance of science and technology makes possible a rational, non-exploitative control of natural resources capable of abolishing scarcity and poverty. What remains to be done, of course, is to create a system of social relations which is equally non-exploitative and on the basis of which men and women can rescue, appropriate and freely develop mankind's cultural heritage. Perhaps the best example of this kind of 'utopian' thinking is this Manifesto written in 2009 in the throes of a popular movement against oppression and exploitation in the French colony of Guadeloupe. It is a document remarkable for its vision of a society with new values, yet at the same time arising directly out of a very concrete situation and movement, a general strike.

Manifesto for 'products of high necessity'
Martinique- Guadeloupe- Guyana- Reunion
(Ernest Breslier, Patrick Chamoiseau, Serge Domi, Gerard Delver, Eduard Delver, Edouard Glissant, Guillaume Pigeard deGurbert, Olivier Portecop, Olivier Pulvar, Jean- Claude William)

At the very moment when the master, the coloniser, proclaims 'there never was a people here', the people who do not exist are a future; it creates itself in the shanty towns and the camps, or in the ghettos in the new conditions of struggle in which a necessarily political art must contribute.

L'image–temps (The time image)

It can only mean one thing: not that there isn't a way out, but that the time has come to abandon the old ways.

It is in full solidarity and without any reservations that we welcome the profound social movement that has gripped Guadeloupe, then Martinique and seems to be spreading to Guyana and Reunion. All our demands are legitimate. None are irrational and certainly none are more excessive than the machinery of the system which they confront. Consequently none of them should be neglected, both for what they represent and for what they imply in relation to all the other demands. The strength of this movement lies in its capacity to organise on a common basis what had remained cut off, been isolated in the blind alleys of specific claims, namely the struggles that had remained inaudible in public administration, the hospitals, the schools, companies, local government, among small craftsmen and the professions…

But the most important is the dynamic of the Lyannaj [the collective representing unions, political parties and associations that led the strike in Guadaloupe] which binds together, rallies, links, connects and relays all the movements that were separate, gives voice to the real suffering of the great mass of people (confronted with a frenzied economic concentration, illegal fiddles and profits), meets diffuse aspirations, which are inexpressible but none the less real, among young people, adults, among the neglected, the invisible, in short all indecipherable suffering parts of our society. Most of them who march en masse discover (or begin to remember) that by taking hold of the impossible by the scruff of the neck, that fatalism can be knocked off its perch.

Consequently, behind the prosaic concern for 'purchasing power' or the 'housewife's shopping basket' looms the essential which evades us and gives meaning to our lives, namely, the poetic. All human life that is fairly balanced will satisfy both the immediate essential needs for survival, food and drink (to put it plainly: the prosaic) and, on the other hand, the aspiration to self-fulfilment nourished by dignity, honour, music, song, sport, dance, reading, philosophy, spirituality, love, leisure time for the satisfaction of one's great innermost desire (to put it plainly: the poetic). As Edgar Morin proposes, living for the sake of living or solely for one's own sake, offers no fulfilment without the life enhancement of what we love and whom we love, of the impossible, of the transcendence to which we all aspire.

'Price inflation' and the 'high cost of living' are not little 'ziguidi' [spirits or demons], devils that leap before us - creatures of spontaneous cruelty cooked up by a few pure-bred 'bekes'[creoles, descendants of white settlers]. They are the creatures of a system red in tooth and claw, ruled over by free market dogma. This dogma now reigns supreme all over the world; it oppresses all the people of the world, it captures their inner lives, their imagination, - resulting not in an 'ethnic cleansing' but in a real 'ethical cleansing' - (that is to say the disenchantment, the removal of all sacred aura and of all symbolic value, even deconstruction) from the human sphere. The system has confined our existence to that of a selfish egotism which closes down all horizons and leaves us no choice but one between the most miserable alternatives: to be either 'consumers' or 'producers.' The consumer only works to consume what his labour power has produced as commodities; and the producer reduces his production to the sole perspective of limitless profit through unlimited phantom-like (phantasmagorical) consumption. The whole system generates what André Gorz describes as antisocial socialisation, where the economic becomes an end in itself to the exclusion of everything else. So when the 'prosaic' does not rise to the level of the 'poetic', when it becomes an end in itself and burns itself out, we tend to believe what we aspire to in our lives, and its need for meaning is to be found in the 'bar codes', our purchasing power and the 'family shopping basket'. Worse still, we end up believing that the virtuous management of the most intolerable misery simply requires a humane and progressive politics. It is therefore a matter of urgency to add to the 'products of bare necessity', the factors that arise starkly from a 'high necessity'.

What then should we count as 'products of high necessity'?

These are at the heart of our painful desire to make ourselves a people and a nation, to enter with dignity on to the world stage, and they are not found at the core of today's negotiations in Martinique and Guadeloupe, and without doubt soon in Guiana and Reunion.

First, no social advances can take place which can only satisfy selfish needs. All social advance can only truly realise itself as a political experience that brings to light the structural lessons of what has taken place. This movement has exposed the tragic institutional disintegration of our countries, the absence of power that could provide a framework. The 'determining' or 'decisive' factor can be secured without trips or telephone calls. Competence only comes with emissaries. Contempt and incompetence reek at every level. Analysis is warped by isolation, blindness and distortion. The farce of the pseudo- powers of the 'Région Département-Prefet', like those of the association of mayors, have shown their impotence, their abject failure when a serious and massive demand arises in a historic cultural entity with a human identity distinct from the ruling metropolitan power, the reality of which has never been treated as such.

And even if such a power solved none of these problems it would at least allow us to address them with full responsibility and to tackle them at last rather than acquiesce in sub-contracting. The question of the beke and the ghettoes that break out here and there are other petty issues that could be solved by an endogenous political authority. The same is true in all respects for the distribution and protection of our land and of the priority to be given to our young people. It is also largely true of our justice system and the fight against the drugs plague.

The lack of responsibility creates bitterness, xenophobia, 'fear of others' and lack of self-confidence. The question of responsibility is therefore one of high necessity.

Then there is the high necessity of understanding that the obscure and inextricable labyrinth of prices, (margins, sub-margins, secret commissions, and obscene profits) is inscribed in the logic of the global free market that has swept over the world with the blind force of a religion. It is also deeply rooted in the colonial absurdity that has estranged us from our country's food and cultural realities, to deliver us naked and without our 'bokay' gardens to European eating habits. It is as if France was forced to import all its foodstuffs and high necessity goods over thousands and thousands of kilometres. To negotiate with the unfathomable chain of operators and middlemen can no doubt bring short-term relief to suffering in the meantime; but the illusory benefits of these arrangements will soon be swept away by the 'market' and all those mechanisms which create a voracious appetite (the drive for profit nourished by 'the colonial spirit' and regulated at a distance) so that the bonuses, freezes, benefits, opportunistic exemptions, and tinkering with dock dues are powerless.

The high necessity is to try right now, without delay, to lay down the foundations of a society that is not ruled by economics, where the notion of development through perpetual growth is replaced by the notion of self-fulfilment; where wages, salaries, consumption and production are synonymous with self-creation and the perfecting of humanity. If capitalism (in its purest form which is its contemporary manifestation) has created this Frankenstein of a consumer, who is nothing more than a basket of commodities, it also engenders wretched 'producers' - bosses, entrepreneurs and other inept professionals who are incapable of any feelings when confronted with upsurges of suffering and the urgent need to imagine another political, economic, social and cultural horizon. In this respect there are no opposite camps. We are all victims of a system that is now blurred, having gone global, which we must confront together. Workers and small employers, consumers and producers, carry within them, somewhere, silent yet irreducible, the high necessity that needs to be awakened, namely the need to live one's life, one's own life, in the constant aspiration to the highest and noblest standards and hence the most fulfilling. Which means living one's life, a life in all the richness of the poetic.

We can bring the system of the market to its knees by a healthy diet and lifestyle.

SARA and the oil companies can sink into oblivion if we use other means of transport than the car.

We can force back the water companies with their exorbitant prices, if we take care of every drop as a precious item to be protected everywhere, to be used as the last few precious gems of a treasure that belonged to everybody.

We cannot defeat or overthrow the prosaic and still live in the cavern of the prosaic. We have to open out the poetic, restraint and sobriety. None of those institutions, however arrogant and powerful (the banks, multinational companies, marketers, or mobile phone operators) could in any way resist this.

Lastly we come to wages and employment.

Here we must determine where lies the high necessity.

Contemporary capitalism reduces wage labour as it increases its production and its profit. Unemployment is a direct consequence of its decreasing need for labour. When factories are relocated it is not because capitalism needs a plentiful labour reserve, but because it wants to cut labour's share even more quickly.

As for the notion of 'full employment', it has been hammered into our imagination by the necessities of industrial development and the ethical cleansing that followed in its wake. Originally labour was inscribed into a symbolic and sacred system (in the political, cultural and personal spheres) which defined its limits and its meaning. Under capitalist rule it lost its creative meaning and its virtue of fulfilment as it became, to the exclusion of everything else, a simple 'job', the only backbone to our days and weeks. Work lost all significance, when having become a simple commodity itself, it ended up by being nothing but access to consumption.

We are now in the depths of the abyss.

There are myriads of talents, creativities, fertile insanities that are sterilised in the corridors of the ANPE (National Employment Agency) and the fenceless camps of structural unemployment born of capitalism. Even when we have got rid of the free market dogma, the technological advances (with soberness and selective de-growth) will help us turn labour value into a kind of rainbow, from the simplest tool to the equation of the highest incandescent creativity. Full employment will not be the child of prosaic productivism, but it will be sought wherever it can initiate new modes of socialisation, autonomous production, in free time and dead time, and can make for solidarity, for sharing, for supporting the destitute, for the ecological restoration of our environment ....

It will be realised in 'whatever makes life worth living'.

There will be civic work and civic income in all that stimulates, which aids dreaming, which leads to meditation, or which opens up to us the delights of lassitude, gives access to music, leads us into the world of books, of the arts, of song, of philosophy, of study, of the high necessity consumption that flowers into creation; creative consumption.

Here is the first basket of demands we bring to the negotiating table and their sequel: that the principle of free access should be posited wherever free access helps people break free from their chains, inspires the imagination, stimulates the cognitive faculties, boosts the creativity, without restraint of the spirit.

Let this principle map out the ways to the books, tales, theatre, music, dancing, the visual arts and crafts, culture and agriculture. Let it be inscribed above the doors of the nursery, primary and secondary schools, colleges and universities, in all the places of learning and development. Let it lead to the creative uses of the new technologies and cyberspace. Let it encourage all that lets us enter into a relation (meetings, contacts, cooperation, interaction and wandering down new paths and ways) with the unforeseeable potentialities of the entire world. It is the principle of free access that allows for a social and cultural politics which determines the fullness of its expectations.

Let us direct our imaginations to the high necessities until the strength of the Lyannaj or of living together, is no longer the 'housewife's shopping basket', but the mass desire for the full development of the idea of humanity.

Let us imagine together a political framework that allows the revitalised societies of Martinique, Guadeloupe, Guyana,

New Reunion taking their sovereign part in the global struggles against capitalism and for a new world ecology.

Let us make the most of this open and living consciousness, so that the negotiations nourish, prolong and open up a flowering across these nations that are truly ours.

We now appeal to those utopias, or a politics that would not be reduced to the management of inadmissible miseries nor the regulation of the savagery of the 'Market', but where it is restored to its essence in the service of all that confers a spirit on the prosaic in surpassing it or putting it to strictly limited use.

We invoke a high politics, a political art, with the individual and the individual's relation to others, at the core of a common project that decrees that life has as its most urgent, intense and most brilliant impulse, the greatest sensitivity to beauty.

This is the 'music of the future', coming from lands distant from Europe and the United States. We should surely be asking how there can be a politics in these 'advanced' capitalist countries which reaches out to these new shoots, to those who struggle against the bitter inheritance of domination by our European Empires. Why cannot their fight for 'products of high necessity' be developed in a fight to overcome and negate the hysterical and dehumanising consumerism of our absurdly overdeveloped Western societies, and asserted against the totalitarian control under which capitalism is developing in China and Russia?

(c) A way forward – utopian?

Everything points to the absolute necessity of a movement against capital which, starting from the felt needs of ordinary people as they come under the hammer of capital (through the IMF, through national governments and through the direct action of big business) trying to deal with its own contradictions by attacking living standards and human rights, becomes international, connecting and mutually enriching by solidarity the resistance struggles which people undertake. From making interconnections between these struggles it will be possible to elaborate and fight for an

International Plan for Development which can anticipate and foreshadow a socialist future not only in the realm of ideas but in practical actions and achievements.

We can here indicate the outline and some of the basic elements of such a plan/programme, as first outlined by David Hookes. It is proposed as a provisional 'programme' which can begin to bring together the problems we have discussed: how the globalisation of capital prepares the conditions for universal intercourse while at the same time distorting and destroying those conditions; how the internet serves capital but is at the same time potentially a weapon in the hands of those who oppose it; how the interests of the peoples of the 'developing' and 'advanced' countries can be united; how and why the necessary revolution is one necessary for the whole of humanity and its future.

Proposal for an International Plan for Development

We live in the era of capitalist globalisation. The market, including the labour market, is global. The ability of national-state economies to make concessions to their 'own' working classes is more and more restricted by their subordination to global movements of capital, and by the absence of any system of political control congruent with the global economy. In place of the working class or proletariat seen by Marx 160 years ago in Britain, Europe and the United States we now see a global working class. It is global, forced into the same global market, but it is divided by nationality, even by mutually opposed immediate interests. The overdevelopment-underdevelopment polarity is paramount in that division of interest. All this, now compounded by the threat to our natural and cultural environment by capital's ruthless and uncontrolled plunder of nature and the bloody wars fought for strategic resources and territory, surely requires that any worthwhile programme, strategy and tactics for the working-class movement and its allies must build towards internationally coordinated action.

Having used the International Monetary Fund to impose attacks (in the name of 'structural adjustment') on the already miserable and oppressive conditions of the peoples of the 'underdeveloped' countries, the major capitalist powers have, especially since the so-called recession of 2008-9,[34] totally abandoned any policies of reform concessions and are actively destroying the welfare gains made in years of struggle. There will inevitably be resistance to these attacks. What is needed, in order to move from a defensive to an offensive strategy is to engage in these movements of resistance, fighting always for ways of achieving temporal and spatial continuity between them as the way to unify them and move from a defensive to an offensive strategy. This must mean developing a programme and forms of organisation which move towards a true working-class internationalism. If this can be done, it will draw in millions of people who are not themselves proletarians, and who, often, do not set out as socialists.

How might a plan for international development become a central part of such a movement? The prospects are not so bleak as might at first appear. Behind the great wealth and power of the big banks and transnational corporations is a gigantic scientific and technological development, especially since the Second World War. It is a development incorporated into capital but it can be the basis of a new leap in humanity's history, instead of its present role as the basis for super-exploitation, the creation of unemployment, the obscene waste of resources through the production of weapons of war that can and do kill millions of people.

The real historical perspective here, and the core of this proposed programme, is what we have called 'the human revolution'. Despite the great threat to our future implicit and explicit in the rule of capital today, we are in fact on the verge of a step change in the evolution of our species. Just as each living organism is a complex interplay of energy and information within a material matrix, so human society, now global, has the need to transcend the acquisitive individualism central to capitalism and

---

[34] In fact it was not a recession in the traditional (conjunctural) sense, but a collapse of the monetarist 'neo-liberal' phase of capitalism's attempts to handle its contradictions, a phase beginning around 1970 and itself an indication of the articulation of the system's structural-historical crisis (see István Mészáros, *Beyond Capital*)

consciously create a truly new social being based on a higher level of integration of energy (distributed solar energy) and global information networks within the material matrix of the biosphere.

In summary, collective social control of the new productive forces could open up the truly human phase of humanity's existence. Instead, the uncontrollable rule of capital is creating the conditions for the annihilation of billions. Its 'information system' is international finance-capital, devoted to the exploitation of humanity and of the resources of nature. Its product is accumulated capital, in particular the 'fictitious capital' at the root of the financial cataclysm of 2008-9.

A programme for the fight against capital – the programme that should be worked towards in the course of every partial struggle – must address this great historical contradiction. This can be done by developing a programme of transitional demands which more and more challenge the existing international order and its national components.

It can take the form of an International Plan for Development.

Such transitional demands would have to be devised in such a way that they can be fought for on an increasingly international scale. There are social movements and political movements (socialist, trade-union, national-liberation, environmentalist, 'anti-capitalist', sustainable development, etc.) which are separated and consequently less effective than if they were united behind a common programme of demands. There will be sectarians who will stand aside on the grounds of ideological correctness, but with every day whatever petty significance they ever had declines. Fixed and dogmatic theoretical positions are the opposite of what must be a living development of theory and of organisational forms adequate to the latest (globalised) stage of capital's development and of the class struggle.

The Plan should strive to link the unemployed in the 'advanced' (overdeveloped) countries with the crisis of poverty, destitution, famine and underdevelopment in the colonial and ex-colonial countries – in other words, attack directly the overdeveloped-underdeveloped polarisation which is so central to capital's rule.

Let the skills of the unemployed be put to work to create the necessary products and technology to arrest and reverse the impoverishment of the masses in Africa, Asia and Latin America.

Already some Intermediate or Appropriate Technology has been developed, on small budgets, by progressive 'alternative' engineers and technologists. Satellite and geosurveying techniques can be combined with appropriate technology on the ground. There are scientists and engineers, together with many young people who could be recruited as volunteers, as experience has shown. Many of them are going to find themselves without job prospects. And equally there are thousands of teachers, nurses and doctors who could be recruited.

Furthermore, such work around the plan will in no sense be in conflict or contradiction with those working for charities in countries like the Sudan, nor, certainly, with those who organise solidarity with the struggles of the Palestinian, Iranian, Kurdish and all other oppressed peoples. The aim must be to integrate all these actions with the work for the Plan. They have the same essential content. And finally

It must be stressed that support will be gained from large numbers of people who are not themselves politically organised, as was shown by the campaign for Workers Aid for Bosnia and Kosova. Thus there is scope for a truly people-wide movement, achieving infinitely more than was ever achieved by any politically concocted 'popular front' policy.

The historical significance of such an initiative will quickly become clear. It reverses the long historical process of denudation of the resources of the colonial and ex-colonial countries – not just the natural resources but, even more important, the human populations (slave labour, the slave trade, peonage and all oppressive forms of labour, including child labour as in today's Africa, where 200 million of children are employed by capitalist firms).

The fight for such a programme/plan will have forms of organisation that enable socialists and others to break from subordination to bureaucratic union apparatuses and bourgeois-national 'liberation' leaders. Thus, instead of popular struggles facilitating the rise of their 'own' capitalist hierarchies, these struggles will be the initiation of an alternative social and economic order, with a true, popular democracy and workers' control as its base. Marxists, for example, would have to adopt a strategy and tactics of engagement with these projects, abandoning the barren perspective of 'building the alternative revolutionary leadership' (themselves, of course).

An immediate objection to such a Plan, inevitably, is that it would have no resources unless financed, presumably by the banks. And here is the Plan's significance for the political struggle in the 'advanced' countries (Britain, Western Europe, the United States, Japan, and soon China and India). There would have to be a political fight (including industrial action) to demand financial resources from taxation. The Copenhagen Accord agreed to set up a fund of $30 billion by 2012, rising o $100 billion by 2020 to enable developing countries to mitigate and adapt to climate change. Political pressure may be able to force use of these resources for the development of projects to link sustainable development in the 'third world' to working communities in Europe and the United States. Pressure and electoral threats could force governments to tax heavily the banks and big business, as well as to abandon expenditure on weapons of war and military campaigns such as in Iraq and Afghanistan.

This is not unrealistic. It is not difficult to envisage, in Britain, for example, that every trade union council, trade union branch, even Labour Party branch, could agree to the eminently rational arguments that could be marshalled for the International Plan for Development. And there are other campaigning and professional organisations (e.g. Scientists for Global Responsibility) who could be expected to agree. Where the established leaders of trade unions and parties like the Labour Party oppose such a proposal they will stand exposed for what they are.

When it becomes possible to set up independent enterprises (small, in the first place) to produce the necessary goods, it is vital that the hierarchical methods of control and division of labour typical of the capitalist factory are replaced by the workforce's own direct control. This would apply to research and development as well as to the direct production process – again anticipating the future.

The Plan should at every stage not be elaborated by an enlightened few and then 'delivered' (see the above chapters on class-consciousness etc), but, on the contrary, drawn up only in collaboration with workers, scientists, engineers, technicians, and peasants and farmers from the countries concerned. Thus we are talking here not about attempts to impose a plan from outside, but rather about a plan for international collaboration.

In the course of elaborating and initiating the implementation of the Plan, the nature and role of those who oppose it (government, political parties, trade union bureaucrats, etc) will become clearer than from any propaganda 'exposure'.

In the first place, the technical proposals will mainly concentrate on appropriate technology for energy, irrigation and transport systems. Generally, parts of the devices can be made locally and parts will require advanced manufacture techniques, a mixture of low-tech and high-tech. Of course, well-founded research programmes would be expected to come up with different mixes of technologies.

It is important that the plan would bring out the potential of the new technologies in harmony with traditional engineering methods. It would also contrast the destructive use under capitalist priorities with their potential under a socialist plan. For example one could point out the following possibility: parallel to ordinary plastic-encapsulated silicon chips there are military ceramic ones. These are intended to withstand extremely harsh (military) environments without failure. They would however be ideal for hardened electronics to control irrigation and energy systems, and would save much human energy expended in 'third world' countries for that purpose.

The Plan for Development campaign could be inked to demands for a non-nuclear energy policy. In particular, we could demand that a properly funded solar energy programme be started. That is the only long-term solution to the energy needs of the world's peoples, that is, the one renewable source that does not heat up the planet. It would not only provide an indigenous source of energy for the impoverished ex-colonies but would provide them with surplus energy to exchange for other necessities.

The campaign would bring into sharp focus the contrast between a scientifically planned, socially controlled solution to economic problems and the destructive chaos of the 'free market'. This contrast would be evident not in the pages of a political tract or manifesto but in a living struggle. It could be seen as the way to rework and bring to life in our changed world the ideas of Marxism, socialism.

The Plan proposal could be raised simultaneously through several trade union councils, initially in areas of high unemployment in Britain such as Merseyside and the North-East. In the Midlands of Britain, for example, there is available expertise in Appropriate Technology (the Centre for Alternative Technology at Machynlleth in mid-Wales) which could be involved. Committees of the trade union councils could be set up to draw up the details of the plan in collaboration with organisations in the colonial and ex-colonial countries. It would be especially important to approach people in those countries which have attempted to establish some independence from imperialism (e.g. Nicaragua, Mozambique, Vietnam, Angola, Namibia, Vietnam, Cuba) and those peoples who have already begun their own fight for independent productive activity (in Brazil, Venezuela, Bolivia, Argentina, the Zapatistas in Mexico, etc.). They will have much to contribute, in practice and in theory. South Africa has a major solar energy programme as well as being a source of radical thinking about the use of the internet (*Ubuntu*, a Zulu word, is becoming the linux dialect of choice for computer operating systems). Venezuela can have a role in promoting and funding alternative technology.

Finally, we may repeat that the already highly developed interconnection (in the interests of capital's functioning) between all spheres of life in the global system, is open to subversion and claim by the forces of resistance and those who would fight for such a Plan and its implementation. The peoples of North Africa, as we have seen, have opened the way. There will, obviously, be many and variegated struggles against the rule of capital everywhere. An International Plan for Development, like every other aspect of these struggles, will need autonomous and interconnected forms of organisation, the internet at the core, and, clearly, not some 'centralised' self-appointed 'vanguard' bringing enlightenment 'from the outside', or from above.

Chapter 13
About Art and Beauty

In an earlier chapter on 'Ends and Means' we stressed the paramount necessity of as clear an understanding as possible of the end to be achieved before devising and engaging in the means to that end. In that light, we need to envisage what might be the meaning of the opening up of a more free and creative life and of our striving towards it. In this chapter I propose that it is in art that we find the highest expression of the struggle to achieve a form of work which overcomes alienation, in which individuals use freedom and the disposable time made possible by the end of the rule of private property in the means of production, and which can reveal a non-exploitative, non-destructive relation between humanity and nature.

This approach is the opposite of the fashion nowadays, which is to ask the age-old questions 'what is art?' or 'what is beauty?' only in a sceptical way, as in 'what is art (beauty) anyway?' and as if to say 'who's to say what I do is not art, is not beautiful?' and so on.

As Mészáros writes about this kind of naïve subjectivism, in his *Marx's Theory of Alienation:* 'The two observed phenomena – the impoverishment of the senses on the one hand, and the endless attacks on the objectivity of aesthetic standards and value on the other – are closely interlinked' (p. 203). That is to say, the question should be taken seriously.

I would call 'art', work (painting, poetry, sculpture, probably music) which opens (reveals) the world (human, natural) and our experience of it to our imagination, so that we see more of the truth of it, we feel more deeply what it has to give.

In his *Ulysses*, James Joyce describes Bloom's reflections on the contrast between the photograph of his wife, 'which did not do justice to her figure', and the National Museum's wonderful Greek statues: 'Marble could give the original, shoulders, back, all the symmetry ... whereas no photo could, because it simply wasn't art in a word.' And in the same novel, Stephen Dedalus pronounces against the false 'realism' of Irish writers who are content to describe only the obvious effects of life under colonial rule.

Paul Klee was surely right: 'Art does not reproduce the visible; rather, it makes visible' (*Creative Credo*, 1920).

As Mikhail Lifshitz, presenting Marx's *Economic and Philosophical Manuscripts*, wrote:

> ... The artist makes his medium speak its own language, thus revealing its inner truth. An aesthetic relation to reality is one of inner organic unity with the object, equally as remote from abstract, contemplative harmony with it as from arbitrary distortion of its own dialectic... (*The Philosophy of Art of Karl Marx* (1933); Pluto Press, 1973)

John Berger in particular has shown that this same relationship is the content of prehistoric cave paintings:

> The first painters were hunters whose lives, like everybody else's in the tribe, depended upon their close knowledge of animals. Yet the act of painting was not the same as the act of hunting: the relation between the two was magical.
>
> In a number of early cave paintings there are stencil representations of the human hand beside the animals. We do not know what precise ritual this served. We do know that painting was used to confirm a magical 'companionship' between prey and hunter, or, to put it more abstractly, between the existent and human ingenuity. Painting was the means of making this companionship explicit and therefore (hopefully) permanent.

Thus

> Every authentic painting demonstrates a collaboration. Look at Petrus Christus' portrait of a young girl in the Staatliche Museum of Berlin, or the stormy seascape in the Louvre by Courbet, or the mouse with an aubergine painted by Tchou-Ta in the seventeenth century, and it is impossible to deny the participation of the model. Indeed, the paintings are not first and foremost about a young woman, a rough sea or a mouse with a vegetable; they are about this participation. 'The brush,' wrote Shitao, the great seventeenth-century Chinese landscape painter, 'is for saving things from chaos.'
>
> It is a strange area into which we are wandering and I'm using words strangely. A rough sea on the northern coast of France, one autumn day in 1870, participating in being seen by a man with a beard who, the following year, will be put in prison! Yet there is no other way of getting close to the actual practice of this silent art, which stops everything moving. (*The Shape of a Pocket*, Vintage International, 2003, pp. 15 & 16)

And another, more familiar, example:

> What do we see? Thyme, other shrubs, limestone rocks, olive trees on a hillside, in the distance a plain, in the sky birds. He dips the pen into brown ink, watches, and marks the paper. The gestures come from his hand, his wrist, arm, shoulder, perhaps even the muscles in his neck, yet the strokes he makes on the paper are following currents of energy which are not physically his and which only become visible when he draws them. (Berger, ibid. p. 89, in the chapter on Vincent Van Gogh)

Here Paul Klee and John Berger greatly advance our understanding of what the artist can reveal about his object. István Mészáros, building on Marx's *Economic and Philosophical Manuscripts*, shows us another, and fundamental, aspect of what enters into the artist's ability to enrich our experience of the natural and historical reality in which we live: '... nature depicted by materialistic artists, often in the most tediously detailed manner, is dehumanised nature.' And on p. 196:

What will determine whether he (the artist) is a realist or not is what he selects from a mass of particular experiences to stand for the given, historically and socially specific, reality. If he is not able to select humanly significant particulars which reveal the fundamental trends and characteristics of the changing human reality, but – for one reason or an other – satisfies himself with depicting reality as it appears to him in its immediacy, no 'faithfulness of detail' will raise him above the level of superficial naturalism. (Istvan Meszaros, *Marx's Theory of Alienation,* Merlin Press, 1970)

What artists convey is what they find in the object, what it makes them feel (Wordsworth, 'emotion recollected in tranquillity'!), and what they communicate, through their art, to their fellow human beings who, past, present and future, have this object as part of their human-transformed/discovered world. The artist's finished work conveys also the concentration of labour and imagination that was necessary to achieve the result. The tradition and heritage of the art are represented and developed at the same time – and these too are part of the struggle that has brought humanity to the point the artist is trying to represent/express.

The exploitation of humans by capital makes impossible a truly human relation to the rest of nature – for the exploiters as well as the exploited. The capitalist cannot 'as individual' or 'as part of human society' participate in the essentially human productive relation to nature without exploiting his fellow-man. The worker has his nature appropriated (in labour time) by the capitalist, and at work is deprived of the initiative and creativity and control which are the distinctively human components of labour.

Humanity is part of nature, its conscious and creative part, able through the work of hand and brain to 'ignite' (Fourier) the slumbering powers of nature. Where capital rules (and, as capital, it initiates and controls production only for its own self-reproduction and accumulation, and so is interested only in exchange-values), this relation is distorted, dehumanised. Ultimately (i.e. in the period we have now entered), the uncontrolled and uncontrollable needs of capital's self-reproduction and growth must become predominantly destructive of nature, including humans ('human nature' properly understood). Perhaps all this is the best way of understanding and explaining what is meant by restoring at a higher level the primitive commune and its community with nature.

The early writings of Marx drive at the same understanding. For example:

> The conception of Nature which prevails under the rule of private property and of money is the practical degradation of Nature .... Contempt for theory, for art, for history, for man ... is the real conscious standpoint and virtue of the moneyed man. (*On the Jewish Question*, 1843)

The understanding of humans' true relation to nature has to be rescued from our society, culture and ideology in which capital rules and the exchange-value of every thing predominates completely over its actual qualities and use-value. The idea that humanity lives by 'exploiting' nature tends to be common to most opponents of capitalism as well as to its proponents.

Taking 'technology' to mean the historically accumulated knowledge and means of production available to humanity, then can we not see artistic production as 'igniting', lighting up, what the world, natural and human, has to give? What we get in the work of art (painting, literature, sculpture, music, etc) is first of all a 'making visible' of what the artist's subject can give (and not just a faithful reproduction of appearances). John Berger has greatly clarified this aspect with his insistence that the artist finds ways to enable the thing portrayed to show its truth against its denaturing – in our day, denaturing by the reduction of things to mere commodities.

I wrote in *Marxism, Ideology and Literature*:

> If (in the society ruled by capital) works of art are deemed possible, must they not rise to the height of inventiveness in finding ways to represent not only what they see but also the necessity of a struggle against the prison of the value form (i.e. of bourgeois society)? (Macmillan, 1980, p. 40.)

In order to be able to do this, the artist can call up the techniques and the inspiration of the artistic culture of the past, including the knowledge of the materials at the artist's disposal. These he not only uses but develops, innovating because the nature and society confronting him have changed and are constantly changing, presenting ever-new challenges.

The work of art has this content, this appeal, as well as giving us deeper insights into what we see. That, it seems to me, is what is meant by 'in the realist work every natural or man-made object must be humanised'. Art is in this way a special part of that essential and unique relation of homo sapiens to the rest of nature: social labour. That is to say, our species relates to nature and evolves, not through inherited instincts and natural selection but in unity with nature through a productive interaction with it. The richness of this relation, the complex struggles and striving involved to wrest its meaning from the exploitation and ideological screens imposed by class society – all this, as well as the image produced to reveal the essence of the thing represented, is contained in the work of art.

This brings us to the most important question of all: the relation between the artist and his/her work, on the one hand, and the life and struggles of his/her fellow-humans on the other. Here I reproduce another passage from my *Marxism, Ideology and Literature*:

> The relation between the form attained by the work of art, on the one hand, and the active struggle through which it was formed, on the other, is one which becomes clear and inspiring to the responsive and aesthetically (musically, or whatever) educated consumer. This success, this experience induced by the artist's work, changes the living man or woman in such a way as to refresh, replenish, develop, perhaps at the same time recall from repressed experience and recognise in himself, the necessary resources to respond to life in a way analogous to the artist's creativity: in the unceasing struggle to make reality correspond to our needs, we must learn both the laws of nature, making them work 'for us', and the special character of social 'laws', whose externality must be dissolved in consciousness into their true element, our own labour, so that the objective possibility of

overcoming them can be envisaged and willed. In this way art goes beyond the imitation of nature, and beyond the labour process as such (p. 58).

Sometimes the heightened feeling and perception stimulated by a work of art is direct and therefore easily explained. I am sure that having seen a painting by Sisley I see an avenue of trees on a country road in France in a richer way and feel more deeply the human relation to nature inherent in the scene (whether I recall at the time the Sisley painting or not). The esplanade at Brighton on a busy summer day seen from a first-floor window looks different and provokes a different feeling if you have loved Pissarro's 'Boulevard Montmartre'. Provençal countryside is not the same if you have not gazed at the paintings of Cézanne or Van Gogh. Leonardo's portraits of women surely enrich your every appreciation of feminine beauty.

Keats' poem 'On first looking into Chapman's Homer' tells us what Chapman's literary art did for him:

Much have I travelled in the realms of gold,
And many goodly states and kingdoms seen;
Round many western islands have I been
Which bards in fealty to Apollo hold.
Oft of one wide expanse had I been told
That deep-brow'd Homer ruled as his demesne;
Yet did I never breathe its pure serene
Till I heard Chapman speak out loud and bold;
Then felt I like some watcher of the skies
When a new planet swims into his ken;
Or like stout Cortes when with eagle eyes
He star'd at the Pacific – and all his men
Look'd at each other with a wild surmise –
Silent, upon a peak in Darien.

But beauty, a beautiful work of art, has more than this 'direct', particular significance. Keats understood this very well. We all know his 'Beauty is truth, truth beauty', but the 'Ode on a Grecian Urn' from which this sentence is taken has more to say that helps us, I think, to understand the role of art and beauty. The last stanza reads:

> O Attic shape! Fair attitude!
> With brede of marble men and maidens overwrought,
> With forest branches and the trodden weed;
> Thou, silent form, dost tease us out of thought
> As doth eternity: Cold Pastoral!
> When old age shall this generation waste,
> Thou shalt remain, in midst of other woe
> Than ours, a friend to man, to whom thou say'st,
> 'Beauty is truth, truth beauty,'
> That is all ye know on earth, and all ye need to know.

These two poems say what I feel needs to be said, but all the same I will try to say in more prosaic fashion what I think we might learn from all this - even if only to drive the reader and myself back to the poems once again, and to look at other literature, paintings and music in the same light.

Here the poet sees the vitality of art, its 'teasing us and future generations out of thought' to accept through a refinement of our senses, our perception, our imagination, what is beautiful and true, what connects us to our fellows, present, past and future in the common struggle to realise our unity with nature. In every age, poetry, painting, music and all artworks are undoubtedly products of their own time, but the artist's struggle to create is one which must find ways to wrest truth from that age and its particular forms of alienation, oppression and ideological deformation. It is in that struggle that artistic innovation is made, and that preserved and rescued (and produced) truth is expressed in forms which enrich the artist's own and future generations.

I can best explain what I think is the necessary starting-point by showing its difference from what I see as a false one. 'Sociology of art and literature', and much that goes by the name of Marxism in this field, fails to get near these essentials, being self-restricted to considerations of how literature and art 'reflect' or 'express' the social conditions in which they were created. The true starting-point is, on the contrary, 'anthropological'. Not in the sense of 'social anthropology', for the most part trapped as it is in a 'structuralist' straitjacket, but in the broad sense of a framework in which the individual human being is a special part of nature, not 'determined' by it and not exploiting it, but relating to the rest of nature by his species' unique capacity for self-creation, for the creation of a 'second nature' (culture). In class society this second nature becomes alienated from him, external to his individual nature and fulfilment, and also separates him from nature itself, which is then considered as something external to him. The capital system is the most complete and general form of this alienation: labour-power itself becomes equatable (as a commodity, for sale, purchase; alienable) to every other commodity. It must be bought and sold for a price (wage) before labour, man's essential being, his active relation to the rest of nature and to his own nature, can even be performed.

Returning then to the first part of this note: the reality (in Sisley's avenue, Pissarro's boulevard, the Mona Lisa or whatever) which the artist discovers and reveals is nature (including of course 'human nature'), to be sure, but it is a nature already not only perceived but also engaged with and changed by humans' own activity, and the portrayal of it shows, includes and furthers the cultivation and refinement of humans' feelings and understanding. And to create in this way is to fight against the existing oppressive and outworn forms of social and artistic life which stand in the way of the individual's freedom and creativity, pointing the way to the time when there will be that freedom, and inspiring us and arming us to get there.

Not everyone will see much point in these remarks about art and beauty or utopia. I cannot resist the temptation to therefore include the following passage from Stendhal's preface to his *De l'Amour* (1822):

> Despite all efforts to be clear and lucid, I cannot perform miracles; I cannot give ears to those who are deaf or eyes to those who are blind. Thus, people with money, who have made 100,000 francs in the year preceding the moment they open this book, must close it quickly, especially if they are bankers, manufacturers, respectable industrialists, that is, eminently practical people. This book will make little sense to

anyone who has made a lot of money on the stock exchange or the lottery. Such a win is not like the habit of passing whole hours in reverie, and enjoying the emotion which comes from a painting by Prud'hon, a passage from Mozart, or, finally, a certain sincere glance from a woman who is often in one's thoughts. People who pay two thousand workers at the end of every week never waste their time in that way. Their spirit always leans to the useful and the practical. The dreamer I am talking about is the man who would hate them if he had the time, and who would not care about being the butt of their jokes. The millionaire industrialist will have the confused feeling that such a man holds a thought in higher esteem than a sack of a thousand francs. (Flammarion, Paris, 1993.)

As already indicated, while it is important to see art as crucial to the potential riches awaiting human beings who will enjoy the creative benefits of 'disposable time' in a communist society ('Cultivated leisure is the aim of man' wrote Oscar Wilde in *The Soul of Man under Socialism*), the creation, understanding and enjoyment of works of art are also fundamental to our responsibility for understanding and changing the society in which we live, including ourselves. Creative artistic work and its products are a direct opposite of the alienation and degradation of labour which are at the heart of the social order dominated by capital, its imperatives and its 'personifications'(Marx). These notes on art and beauty would not be out of place in the earlier chapter on alienation of labour.

We may approach this aspect once again via Marx's well-known chapter on the labour-process:

We presuppose labour in a form that stamps it as exclusively human. A spider conducts operations that resemble those of a weaver, and a bee puts to shame many an architect in the construction of her cells. But what distinguishes the worst architect from the best of bees is this, that the architect raises his structure in imagination before he erects it in reality. At the end of every labour-process, we get a result that already existed in the imagination of the labourer at its commencement. He not only effects a change of form in the material on which he works, but he also realises a purpose of his own that gives the law to his modus operandi, and to which he must subordinate his will. (*Capital*, Vol. 1 Part 3.)

In his own way, Cézanne knew that work must have this conscious, creative drive; 'One must be a good worker... The ideal of earthly happiness – to have a good formula'. (Quoted by Max Raphael in *The Demands of Art*, Routledge, 1968, p. 43)

Artistic work is a struggle to find ways of expressing man's true relation to nature and to himself, against the prevailing alienation. Capital exploits and plunders nature, it exploits man's fundamental relation to nature, which is creative labour, a creative labour needing to husband nature, not exploit and plunder it. Nature's creations are exploited and distorted, torn from their living, renewable source; humans are exploited and distorted, torn (alienated) from their natural and social relations, their fellow-humans; the relation between humans (creative labour and its mutual benefits) is exploited and distorted.

The artist fights, in his own way, against this alienation, exploitation, distortion, disfigurement, and for the truth, against a mode of production in which that truth is lost.

In the society ruled by capital, the parts of nature encountered and transformed by human labour relate to one another, and to their producers and users, not as the mutually related realisations of a truly human relation between humanity and nature and between humans, but only as exchange-values, repositories of value to be realised on 'the market'. Their relations are quantifiable (via money) but with no intrinsic connection between their natural-historical characteristics.

The artist's work – the process and the result – is to re-assert creativity against this order of things, resisting it, criticising it, insisting on the construction (literary, pictorial, architectural, musical, plastic, etc) of a whole, in which the parts are restored to their true relationships, that is to say, differently ('beautifully') from the distorted relations between the parts of our social/cultural order. Whether this is done musically, pictorially, poetically, etc, depends on the artist's own talents, abilities and individual experiences as part of his social milieu. This is the only true 'realism', to point to and reveal the natural/historical-cultural reality hidden and distorted by the blinding commodification and alienation. The true work of art is a recognition and exposure of the enemy, and it should be no surprise if, against the commercialism and corruption of his society, the artist embraces 'art for art's sake'. Again Cézanne: 'The day will come when one carrot painted with originality will be pregnant with revolution.'!

In his *The Demands of Art*, Max Raphael, in the course of a detailed analysis of one of Cézanne's most famous paintings (Mont Sainte-Victoire, 1904-06), summarises the content of the work of art as understood in the above terms: '... the work of art holds man's creative powers in a crystalline suspension from which it can again be transformed into living energies' (p. 187), and:

> [We must] view art as a productive act which dissolves frozen, reified elements and gives permanent form to this process by combining opposites into unity. Art, to the extent that it creates true insights into nature and society, is one of the highest forms of the creative forces that dominate nature, society and the mind, and every work of art contains within it spiritual energies, the release of which can increase our own productive capacity. Our sense of human dignity is enhanced when we employ the energies released by our creative analysis of art for the cultivation of nature, for the development of personality, and for shaping a more just society. (p. 189)

And finally:

> Creative instinct manifests itself with greater freedom in art than in any other domain. A creative, active study of art is therefore indispensable to awaken creative powers, to assert them against the dead weight of tradition, and to mobilise them in the struggle for a social order in which everyone will have the fullest opportunity to develop his creative capacities. The details of this social order cannot be anticipated without falling into utopian dreams. We can and must be satisfied

with the awareness that art helps us to achieve the truly just order. The decisive battles, however, will be fought at another level. (p. 204)

Chapter 14
By way of conclusions

Stendhal (recalling his thoughts of the year 1811), wrote: 'I have always, as it were by some instinct, profoundly despised the bourgeois .... So then, according to me, energy was only to be found, in my opinion [in 1811], in that class which has to struggle with real needs.'[35] In its own way an anticipation of Karl Marx, in a passage directly related to our concern with 'agency': 'Theory becomes a material force as soon as it grips the masses ... Theory can be realised in a people only insofar as it is the realisation of the needs of that people.'[36]

István Mészáros, asked in an interview with the journal *Radical Change* (1992) if he thought the working class was still the agent of revolutionary change, replied:

> Undoubtedly, there cannot be any other. I remember there was a time when Herbert Marcuse was dreaming about the new social agents, the intellectuals and the outcasts, but neither of them had the power to implement change. The intellectuals can play an important role in defining strategies, but it cannot be that the outcasts are the force which implements this change. The only force which can introduce this change and make it work is society's producers, who have the repressed energies and potentialities through which all these problems and contradictions can be solved. The only agency which can rectify this situation, which can assert

---

[35] Stendhal, *Life of Henry Brulard*, Penguin Classics, 1973, p. 34
[36] Marx, 'Contribution to Critique of Hegel's Philosophy of Law. Introduction', in Marx and Engels *Collected Works*, Vol.3, p. 183

itself, and find fulfilment in the process of asserting itself, is the working class.[37]

In this book, we have tried to face up to the difficult questions which this assertion raises not only for Marxists but for all those who recognise the need for fundamental social change from a system – the rule of capital – which threatens the whole future of our children and our children's children. Can Marx's main ideas about the fight for socialism, and the social force which will conduct that fight, apply in today's greatly changed conditions?

Those conclusions were:

1. Capitalism develops the productive forces and means of universal intercourse to the level sufficient for a socialist society.
2. Capital's basic metabolism is based on the exploitation of wage- labour, 'the theft of alien labour time'. This mode of production comes into contradiction with the highly developed productive forces.
3. Capital creates its own 'gravediggers', its structural antagonist, the working class.
4. Marx and Engels therefore end the *Communist Manifesto*: 'Workers of the world, unite! You have nothing to lose but your chains.'

What questions, then?

On 1: There has indeed been an enormous development of productive forces and of the means of universal intercourse. BUT capital's development, its self-reproduction, is no longer simply providing mankind with a sufficient basis for socialism. It has become destructive in the extreme, destructive of nature and of culture. Its destruction of the environment and of culture are now undermining and corrupting the elementary necessary preconditions for a socialist order. It is surely not enough to respond by saying, 'That makes more urgent the necessity to end

---

[37] Reprinted in Mészáros, *Beyond Capital*, p. 984

capitalism'. How is it to be ended? How are these endangered preconditions to be defended?

On 2: The contradiction has been dominating all social life for more than a century. It has given rise to a number of economic crises. Until the recent financial collapse (2008-9) the most serious of these was the crash of 1929 and the subsequent Depression. Imperialist expansion and export of capital, world wars, post-war reconstruction booms, fascist regimes, and welfare state systems, together with the betrayal of several working-class revolutions, enabled capitalism to export, attenuate or displace its contradictions in the twentieth century. By the 1970s these mechanisms became decreasingly possible, and the capital system entered its phase of structural crisis. At this point, on the basis of the expansion achieved by the above means, there was a return to the unbridled market, monetarism, 'neo-liberalism'.

Now that last phase has led to the collapse of the financial system and massive 'sovereign debt', with, now beginning, disastrous effects on the 'real economy' (closures, bankruptcies, mass unemployment).

None of the mechanisms for displacing contradictions in the last century are available. Thus today's crisis is more than a 'recession', with a presumed 'recovery'.

Certain measures may be found to delay the progress of this crisis, but we may well have come to the end of that historical period in which capital could find ways of displacing its main contradiction by adopting temporary neo-Keynesian policies.

On 3: As always, capital cannot exist without the existence of a class of men and women with no means of production of their own, forced to sell their labour-power. This working class is far, far bigger than it was in Marx's day, and with the 'globalisation' of capital the proletariat exists in every country in the world.

Within this massive proletarianisation there are other changes.

(a) The workers of the 'advanced capitalist countries' (Western Europe, North America and Japan) are far outnumbered by the working classes of China, the ex-Soviet Union, the Indian sub-continent and Latin America. In China and the ex-Soviet Union, workers confront a capitalist class which has great differences from those confronted by workers in Marx's day and from those confronting the workers of the USA and Western

Europe. For example, Chinese capitalists are at the same time inheritors of a totalitarian state apparatus, and there is in Chinese industry a massive presence of capital invested by American and European transnational companies, some of it directly, under state licence, some of it jointly with Chinese capitalists, some of it in joint enterprises with the state.

(b) At the same time, the internal composition of the working class in the older capitalist countries has greatly changed. Workers in the so-called service industries now outnumber those in manufacturing.

(c) The growing proportion of structural unemployment means that large numbers of working-class families are condemned to a prospect of never again having someone in paid employment. Insofar as they are unlikely ever again to be in work, their membership of a working class structurally necessary to capital and hence its 'structural antagonist' becomes questionable (this was not the case where the unemployed were a 'reserve army of labour'); on the contrary they are a burden on the system. They become dependent on state benefits and/or 'fiddling' of various sorts. They live in badly deprived areas in which drugs and crime are rampant. These are some of the social-pathological consequences of the structural crisis or overdevelopment in the older capitalist countries.

In every continent, there are millions of men and women who are proletarians, in the sense that they are impoverished, dispossessed and disempowered; but they are not employed, and so not structurally essential to capital. The relation between the employed working class and these other proletarians is a highly important question.

On 4: The working class in the older capitalist countries is disfranchised. There are no working-class political parties. Trade unions organise only a tiny proportion of workers (in Britain, for example, 12 per cent). Furthermore, while the framework of politics within which the working class can engage is still a national one, this national framework of politics is in no way congruent with today's globalised economy. How will the working class and it allies (the dispossessed, peasants, intellectuals) be able to organise against global capital? How will the workers of

Western Europe and the USA, for example, find ways to overcome competition with Chinese workers, and organise together with them? The success of organised resistance by use of the internet and mobile phone in China (and Russia) suggests possibilities.

It is vitally important to stress that we do not yet know what forms of struggle and organisation will come into existence as the capital system's crisis and its destructiveness of nature and culture affect the people of every country on the planet. These must be studied, engaged with and learned from, and on no account approached with set, dogmatic formulae learned in another epoch. In particular, it is imperative to avoid like the plague all notions of a pre-written prescription for 'revolutionary class consciousness', to be delivered to the working class by some self-appointed 'leadership' which 'intervenes' to 'politicise' each partial struggle. All notions of the relation between spontaneous struggles and political consciousness brought 'from the outside' must be forgotten – we do not even know what those spontaneous struggles will be or with what self-consciousness. We have to learn from what Marx called 'the real movement', and it will be a real movement very different from what it was in the nineteenth or the twentieth centuries.

The first 'human revolution' (see above Chapter 8, 'The human revolution ... and the modern family?) was the transition from pre-human to human. In the earliest human communities, which were very small, there was collective, shared labour, with sharing of the fruits and the rule of reciprocity: a form of communism.

In the course of time, a surplus product became possible. There were different forms of utilising and sharing the surplus, but eventually surplus product and means of production could be privately appropriated and used for the exploitation and domination of the labour of others, including the male domination and exploitation of women in the patriarchal and monogamous families. The state came into existence to protect private property and to control the class of dispossessed.

The last of the class societies which developed was (is) the system ruled by capital. We can see the history of class societies as a long and contradictory process of counter-revolution, negating the first human revolution. To say that the process is contradictory means that along with the exploitation, the hierarchical and iniquitous division of labour, and the class conflict and oppression goes a development of mankind's productive forces.

This negation, this counter-revolution, reaches its extreme form in the capitalist mode of production. With capitalism, a profound change comes about. Capital's very mode of existence is one of continuous self-reproduction and accumulation. It is a self-reproductive process which necessarily stimulates a development of productive forces. This development always had its destructive as well as progressive results, but by the twentieth century capital's mode of self-reproduction began to be predominantly destructive, of nature itself as well as of culture.

Having already resulted in a development of productive forces to a level necessary for the material foundations of a truly human society, the survival of capitalism now became destructive of those foundations. Overcoming, surpassing, the rule of capital now becomes an urgent necessity for our future. Capital's negation of the first human revolution must now itself be negated. That will be our human revolution; not just a human revolution 'like' the first one, but the overcoming (negating) of all the negations of that first one. A dialectical method is all-important. It is a gem of philosophy that 'comparison is not the same thing as reason'.

What must be uncovered in every case are not comparisons but the interconnections, contradictory processes and 'laws of motion' of the things we seek to understand and act upon.

Some maxims for the above:

'Dialectics ... the science of interconnnections' (Engels)

'Comparison is not Reason'

'The philosophers have interpreted the world. The problem, however, is to change it.' (Marx)

'Since it is in the nature of tradition to incorporate false statements we must examine the causes which produce them. They are:

(a) attachment to certain opinions and schools of thought. Now if a man's mind is impartial in receiving tradition he examines it with all due care so that he can distinguish between the true and the false; but if he is pervaded by attachment to any particular opinion or sect he immediately accepts any tradition which supports it; and this tendency and attachment cloud his judgment so that he is unable to criticize and scrutinize what he hears, an straightway accepts what is false and hands it on to others;

(b) over-confidence in the probity of those who hand on the tradition;

(c) ignorance of the real significance of events; for many traditionists, now knowing the significance of what they saw and heard, record events together with their own interpretations or conjectures and so give false information;

(d) belief that one has the truth. This is widespread and comes generally from over-confidence in narrators of the past;

(e) ignorance of the circumstances surrounding an event induced byd ambiguity or embellishment. The narrator hands on the story as he understands it with these misleading and false elements'. (Ibn Khaldun, 14th-century writer on the philosophy of history)

INDEX

A

Africa xiv, 10-16, 27, 118, 119, 137, 138,155, 156, 159
Alienation 37, 39, 64, 69, 73-76, 89, 121, 128, 162-172
'Arab spring' 119

B

Balzac, Honoré de 130
Benjamin, Walter 44, 52,59, 122, 141
Berger, John 162-5
Broué, Pierre 130
Bush, George W. 40

C

Cameron, David 120
Camus, Albert 8
Carey, Peter 139
Cézanne, Paul 171ff
Chesnais, François 24, 25
China, 6, 12-19, 25, 32-38, 42, 51-69, 88, 104, 117, 123, 126, 127, 134, 138, 152, 157, 177, 179
Class-consciousness 20, 105, 132-136, 157
Climate change 157

Communist Manifesto 2, 50, 108, 126, 130, 176
Courbet, Gustave 163
Crime 26, 32, 33, 39, 41,42, , 43, 66, 134, 178
Cultural revolution 123

D

Davis, Mike 135
De Lillo, Don 69
Debt 13, 24, 36, 61, 1, 37, 61, 119, 137, 177, 183
Destructive self-reproduction vii, 4, 26, 70, 112

E

ecological crisis 9, 10, 18, 57
enclosures 41, 42
Engels, Frederick 2, 25, 32-34, 45, 51, 71, 77, 87, 86, 90, 95-98, 100-103, 109, 126, 176, 180
ethnic cleansing 30, 147
Eurozone 24

F

Facebook 49
family xvi, 20, 87-99, 147, 179
fascism 12, 18, 45

fictitious capital 17, 24, 61, 155,
Fourier, Charles 51, 122, 164
Fourth International 124, 134
Fox, Liam 120
Friedman, Milton 16, 40

G

General Strike, Britain 12
Globalisation x, 1, 5, 16-17, 23, 24, 35, 50, 52, 63, 88, 109, 119, 153, 177
Gorz, André 146
Gove, Michael 120
Gramsci Antonio viii, 131
Greece 25, 119
Grossman, Vasily 26, 43, 123
Guadeloupe 144ff
Guthrie, Woody 41

H

Hayek, Friedrich von 16
Hegel, Friedrich 100, 107
Hilferding, Rudolph 23,
Hutton, Will 68

I

Intellectuals 30, 45, 108, 110, 117, 130-133, 174, 178,181, 185
Internet, IT, etc. 1, 15, 35, 48, 49, 89, 110-117, 153, 159,179
Iran 42
Iraq 6, 39, 42, 43, 122, 143, 157, 163

J

Joyce, James 161

K

Keats, John 167
Keynes, John Maynard 16, 18, 25, 177
Kissinger, Henry 42
Klee, Paul 162, 163
Klein, Naomi 40,
Kurds, Kurdistan 42

L

Larkin, Joe 144
Lassalle, Ferdinand 128
Lawrence, D.H. ix, x
Leach, Edmund 99
Lenin, Vladimir xviii, 7, 11, 25, 27, 28, 35, 45, 123-126,130, 133, 138
Lessing, Doris 116
Lifshitz, Evgeny 162
Lukacs, Georg xviii, 132-138,
Luxemburg, Rosa 11, 44

M

MacGregor, David 84
Marxism, Ideology and Literature (Slaughter) 165,166
Meszaros, Istvan xi, xviii, 6, 18, 26, 27n, 34, 57, 58, 65, 67, 107, 121, 132, 133, 161, 164, 174
Michel, Louise 144
More, Thomas 141

Morgan, Lewis Henry 91, 92, 96
Morin, Edgar 146

N

Nechaev, Sergei 123
Negt, Oskar 113-119,
neo-liberalism 16, 177
New Orleans 40, 43
Nixon, Richard 42
Not Without a Storm
(Slaughter) 26, 49, 107

O

'Occupy' 118,119
Odets, Clifford 135
Orwell, George 131
outlook of political economy 102, 105
overdevelopment xiv, 23ff, 50, 68, 69, 90, 95, 117, 153, 178
Owen, Robert 51

P

Paris Commune 126, 144
party and class 135
Petrus Christus 163
Pissarro, Camille 167, 169
Potter, Denis 109, 110

R

Raoul 130, 134
Raphael, Max 171, 172
revolutionary agency 101ff
Ricardo, David 101
Rosdolsky, Roman 57

Russia 12, 36, 89, 94, 132, 133, 159, 185

S

Saint-Simon 52, 122, 141
Sarkozy, Nicolas 30, 39
Second World War 12, 17, 26, 27, 125, 154
Seeger, Pete 41
Sisley, Alfred 167, 169
Smith, Adam 101
'social brain' 47-64, 68, 77, 79, 83, 91, 94
social revolution 52, 101, 102, 105, 128, 135,
Social-democracy 17, 28, 46
socialisation of production 47ff, 94, 95, 147
'socialism in one country' 123, 124
socialism or barbarism' 44
sociology 168
Spanish civil war 12
Stalin, Joseph 123
Stalinism 7, 11, 15-20, 32, 35, 44, 46, 123, 124, 130-134
Stendhal 169, 175
Strindberg, August 99
structural crisis 7, 13-18, 27, 45, 79, 87, 88, 113, 118, 119

T

Thatcher, Margaret 2, 16, 17, 24, 25, 32, 41, 90, 99
Tiananmen Square 35
Tiedemann, Rolf 44
time, free time, 1, 4, 5, 8, 29, 39, 48-59, 63ff, 77. 79. 83,

88, 145, 151, 161, 164, 170, 176
Trotsky Leon xviii, 11, 12, 25, 28, 123-138
Trotskyism 125, 130, 131, 134
Twitter 49

U

'underclass' 19
Unemployment xv, 7, 18, 24, 28, 35, 65, 79, 118, 150, 154 159, 177, 178

V

Van Gogh, Vincent 163, 167
Vollmar, Georg von 124

W

Wainwright, Hilary 113
welfare state 12, 31, 37, 109, 138, 177
Wheen, Francis 42
Wilde, Oscar 99, 170
Wollstonecraft, Mary 98
Wordsworth, William 164